Modern Critical Interpretations

Zora Neale Hurston's
Their Eyes Were Watching God

Modern Critical Interpretations

The Oresteia
Beowulf
The General Prologue to
   The Canterbury Tales
The Pardoner's Tale
The Knight's Tale
The Divine Comedy
Exodus
Genesis
The Gospels
The Iliad
The Book of Job
Volpone
Doctor Faustus
The Revelation of St.
   John the Divine
The Song of Songs
Oedipus Rex
The Aeneid
The Duchess of Malfi
Antony and Cleopatra
As You Like It
Coriolanus
Hamlet
Henry IV, Part I
Henry IV, Part II
Henry V
Julius Caesar
King Lear
Macbeth
Measure for Measure
The Merchant of Venice
A Midsummer Night's
   Dream
Much Ado About
   Nothing
Othello
Richard II
Richard III
The Sonnets
Taming of the Shrew
The Tempest
Twelfth Night
The Winter's Tale
Emma
Mansfield Park
Pride and Prejudice
The Life of Samuel
   Johnson
Moll Flanders
Robinson Crusoe
Tom Jones
The Beggar's Opera
Gray's Elegy
Paradise Lost
The Rape of the Lock
Tristram Shandy
Gulliver's Travels

Evelina
The Marriage of Heaven
   and Hell
Songs of Innocence and
   Experience
Jane Eyre
Wuthering Heights
Don Juan
The Rime of the Ancient
   Mariner
Bleak House
David Copperfield
Hard Times
A Tale of Two Cities
Middlemarch
The Mill on the Floss
Jude the Obscure
The Mayor of
   Casterbridge
The Return of the Native
Tess of the D'Urbervilles
The Odes of Keats
Frankenstein
Vanity Fair
Barchester Towers
The Prelude
The Red Badge of
   Courage
The Scarlet Letter
The Ambassadors
Daisy Miller, The Turn
   of the Screw, and
   Other Tales
The Portrait of a Lady
Billy Budd, Benito Cer-
   eno, Bartleby the Scriv-
   ener, and Other Tales
Moby-Dick
The Tales of Poe
Walden
Adventures of
   Huckleberry Finn
The Life of Frederick
   Douglass
Heart of Darkness
Lord Jim
Nostromo
A Passage to India
Dubliners
A Portrait of the Artist as
   a Young Man
Ulysses
Kim
The Rainbow
Sons and Lovers
Women in Love
1984
Major Barbara

Man and Superman
Pygmalion
St. Joan
The Playboy of the
   Western World
The Importance of Being
   Earnest
Mrs. Dalloway
To the Lighthouse
My Antonia
An American Tragedy
Murder in the Cathedral
The Waste Land
Absalom, Absalom!
Light in August
Sanctuary
The Sound and the Fury
The Great Gatsby
A Farewell to Arms
The Sun Also Rises
Arrowsmith
Lolita
The Iceman Cometh
Long Day's Journey Into
   Night
The Grapes of Wrath
Miss Lonelyhearts
The Glass Menagerie
A Streetcar Named
   Desire
Their Eyes Were
   Watching God
Native Son
Waiting for Godot
Herzog
All My Sons
Death of a Salesman
Gravity's Rainbow
All the King's Men
The Left Hand of
   Darkness
The Brothers Karamazov
Crime and Punishment
Madame Bovary
The Interpretation of
   Dreams
The Castle
The Metamorphosis
The Trial
Man's Fate
The Magic Mountain
Montaigne's Essays
Remembrance of Things
   Past
The Red and the Black
Anna Karenina
War and Peace

These and other titles in preparation

Zora Neale Hurston's
Their Eyes Were Watching God

Edited and with an introduction by

Harold Bloom
Sterling Professor of the Humanities
Yale University

Chelsea House Publishers
NEW YORK ◇ PHILADELPHIA

© 1987 by Chelsea House Publishers,
a subsidiary of Haights Cross Communications.

Introduction © 1986 by Harold Bloom

Printed and bound in the United States of America

10   9

∞ The paper used in this publication meets the minimum
requirements of the American National Standard for
Permanence of Paper for Printed Library Materials,
Z39.48-1984.

Library of Congress Cataloging-in-Publication Data
Zora Neal Hurston's Their eyes were watching God.
   (Modern critical interpretations)
   Bibliography: p.
   Includes index.
   1. Hurston, Zora Neale. Their eyes were watching God. 2.
Afro-American women in literature.
I. Bloom, Harold.   II. Series.
PS3515.U789T639   1987   813'.52   86-34320
ISBN 1-55546-054-2 (alk. paper)

Contents

785607

Editor's Note

This book gathers together the best criticism available upon Zora Neale Hurston's *Their Eyes Were Watching God*. The critical essays are reprinted here in the chronological order of their original publication. I am grateful to Bernice Hausman and Henry Finder for their aid in editing this volume.

My introduction centers upon the heroic vitalism that constitutes both the author's and the heroine's stance, both experiential and rhetorical. Robert B. Stepto begins the chronological sequence of criticism with his brief but influential account of *Their Eyes*, which he considers as an ascent and immersion pattern of narrative. A manifesto for black feminist criticism, Lorraine Bethel's essay finds in the novel a "black woman–identified bonding" that some readers cannot locate, and may continue to overlook. Missy Dehn Kubitschek sees Janie as a quest figure and part of a vision of "group ascent," an element in the narrative that again some readers may fail to discover.

Houston A. Baker, Jr., attempting an "ideological analysis," dismisses the romance elements in Hurston's story, and gives us instead a case study of mercantile economics and the black author's financial dilemmas. In a very different deconstruction, inspired by the work of Paul de Man, Barbara Johnson provides a rigorous rhetorical analysis that shows the extraordinary strength of Hurston's rhetorical art. More generally, Elizabeth Meese studies the relation between Janie's voice and Hurston's transformation of other texts into her own (in Meese's view) feminist stance.

This volume concludes with two previously unpublished contributions. Barbara Johnson returns, with the eminent Henry Louis Gates, Jr., in an exegesis of the shifts in the idiom of Hurston's authorial voice. Finally, John F. Callahan grants us a full-scale reading of the novel in which a call-and-response form is uncovered, one in which "aesthetic intimacy" is achieved through a collaboration of voices.

Introduction

Extra-literary factors have entered into the process of even secular canon-
ization from Hellenistic Alexandria into the High Modernist Era of Eliot
and Pound, so that it need not much dismay us if contemporary work by
women and by minority writers becomes esteemed on grounds other than
aesthetic. When the High Modernist critic Hugh Kenner assures us of the
permanent eminence of the novelist and polemicist Wyndham Lewis, we
can be persuaded, unless of course we actually read books like *Tarr* and
Hitler. Reading Lewis is a rather painful experience, and makes me skeptical
of Kenner's canonical assertions. In the matter of Zora Neale Hurston, I
have had a contrary experience, starting with skepticism when I first en-
countered essays by her admirers, let alone by her idolators. Reading *Their
Eyes Were Watching God* dispels all skepticism. *Moses: Man of the Mountain*
is an impressive book in its mode and ambitions, but a mixed achievement,
unable to resolve problems of diction and of rhetorical stance. Essentially,
Hurston is the author of one superb and moving novel, unique not in its
kind but in its isolated excellence among other stories of the kind.

The wistful opening of *Their Eyes Were Watching God* pragmatically
affirms greater repression in women as opposed to men, by which I mean
"repression" only in Freud's sense: unconscious yet purposeful forgetting:

> Now, women forget all those things they don't want to re-
> member, and remember everything they don't want to forget.
> The dream is the truth. Then they act and do things accordingly.

Hurston's Janie is now necessarily a paradigm for women, of whatever
race, heroically attempting to assert their own individuality in contexts that
continue to resent and fear any consciousness that is not male. In a larger
perspective, should the contexts modify, the representation of Janie will

take its significant place in a long tradition of such representations in English and American fiction. This tradition extends from Samuel Richardson to Doris Lessing and other contemporaries, but only rarely has been able to visualize authentically strong women who begin with all the deprivations that circumstance assigns to Janie. It is a crucial aspect of Hurston's subtle sense of limits that the largest limitation is that imposed upon Janie by her grandmother, who loves her best, yet fears for her the most.

As a former slave, the grandmother, Nanny, is haunted by the compensatory dream of making first her daughter, and then her granddaughter, something other than "the mule of the world," customary fate of the black woman. The dream is both powerful enough, and sufficiently unitary, to have driven Janie's mother away, and to condemn Janie herself to a double disaster of marriages, before the tragic happiness of her third match completes as much of her story as Hurston desires to give us. As readers, we carry away with us what Janie never quite loses, the vivid pathos of her grandmother's superb and desperate displacement of hope:

> "And, Janie, maybe it wasn't much, but Ah done de best Ah kin by you. Ah raked and scraped and bought dis lil piece uh land so you wouldn't have to stay in de white folks' yard and tuck yo' head befo' other chillun at school. Dat was all right when you was little. But when you got big enough to understand things, Ah wanted you to look upon yo'self. Ah don't want yo' feathers always crumpled by folks throwin' up things in yo' face. And Ah can't die easy thinkin' maybe de menfolks white or black is makin' a spit cup outa you: Have some sympathy fuh me. Put me down easy, Janie, Ah'm a cracked plate."

II

Hurston's rhetorical strength, even in *Their Eyes Were Watching God,* is frequently too overt, and threatens an excess, when contrasted with the painful simplicity of her narrative line and the reductive tendency at work in all her characters except for Janie and Nanny. Yet the excess works, partly because Hurston is so considerable and knowing a mythologist. Hovering in *Their Eyes Were Watching God* is the Mosaic myth of deliverance, the pattern of revolution and exodus that Hurston reimagines as her prime trope of power:

> But there are other concepts of Moses abroad in the world. Asia and all the Near East are sown with legends of this character.

They are so numerous and so varied that some students have come to doubt if the Moses of the Christian concept is real. Then Africa has her mouth on Moses. All across the continent there are the legends of the greatness of Moses, but not because of his beard nor because he brought the laws down from Sinai. No, he is revered because he had the power to go up the mountain and to bring them down. Many men could climb mountains. Anyone could bring down laws that had been handed to them. But who can talk with God face to face? Who has the power to command God to go to a peak of a mountain and there demand of Him laws with which to govern a nation? What other man has ever commanded the wind and the hail? The light and darkness? That calls for power, and that is what Africa sees in Moses to worship. For he is worshipped as a god.

Power in Hurston is always *potentia,* the demand for life, for more life. Despite the differences in temperament, Hurston has affinities both with Dreiser and with Lawrence, heroic vitalists. Her art, like theirs, exalts an exuberance that is beauty, a difficult beauty because it participates in reality-testing. What is strongest in Janie is a persistence akin to Dreiser's Carrie and Lawrence's Ursula and Gudrun, a drive to survive in one's own fashion. Nietzsche's vitalistic injunction, that we must try to live as though it were morning, is the implicit basis of Hurston's true religion, which in its American formulation (Thoreau's), reminds us that only that day dawns to which we are alive. Something of Lawrence's incessant sense of the sun is paralleled by Hurston's trope of the solar trajectory, in a cosmos where: "They sat on the boarding house porch and saw the sun plunge into the same crack in the earth from which the night emerged" and where: "Every morning the world flung itself over and exposed the town to the sun."

Janie's perpetual sense of the possibilities of another day propels her from Nanny's vision of safety first to the catastrophe of Joe Starks and then to the love of Tea Cake, her true husband. But to live in a way that starts with the sun is to become pragmatically doom-eager, since mere life is deprecated in contrast to the possibility of glory, of life more abundant, rather than Nanny's dream of a refuge from exploitation. Hurston's most effective irony is that Janie's drive toward her own erotic potential should transcend her grandmother's categories, since the marriage with Tea Cake is also Janie's pragmatic liberation from bondage toward men. When he tells her, in all truth, that she has the keys to the kingdom, he frees her from living in her grandmother's way.

A more pungent irony drove Hurston to end Janie's idyll with Tea Cake's illness and the ferocity of his subsequent madness. The impulse of her own vitalism compels Janie to kill him in self-defense, thus ending necessarily life and love in the name of the possibility of more life again. The novel's conclusion is at once an elegy and a vision of achieved peace, an intense realization that indeed we are all asleep in the outer life:

> The day of the gun, and the bloody body, and the courthouse came and commenced to sing a sobbing sigh out of every corner in the room; out of each and every chair and thing. Commenced to sing, commenced to sob and sigh, singing and sobbing. Then Tea Cake came prancing around her where she was and the song of the sigh flew out of the window and lit in the top of the pine trees. Tea Cake, with the sun for a shawl. Of course he wasn't dead. He could never be dead until she herself had finished feeling and thinking. The kiss of his memory made pictures of love and light against the wall. Here was peace. She pulled in her horizon like a great fish-net. Pulled it from around the waist of the world and draped it over her shoulder. So much of life in its meshes! She called in her soul to come and see.

III

Hurston herself was refreshingly free of all the ideologies that currently obscure the reception of her best book. Her sense of power has nothing in common with politics of any persuasion, with contemporary modes of feminism, or even with those questers who search for a black esthetic. As a vitalist, she was of the line of the Wife of Bath and Sir John Falstaff and Mynheer Peeperkorn. Like them, she was outrageous, heroically larger than life, witty in herself and the cause of wit in others. She belongs now to literary legend, which is as it should be. Her famous remark in response to Carl Van Vechten's photographs is truly the epigraph to her life and work: "I love myself when I am laughing. And then again when I am looking mean and impressive." Walt Whitman would have delighted in that as in her assertion: "When I set my hat at a certain angle and saunter down Seventh Avenue . . . the cosmic Zora emerges. . . . How *can* any deny themselves the pleasure of my company? It's beyond me." With Whitman, Hurston herself is now an image of American literary vitality, and a part also of the American mythology of exodus, of the power to choose the party of Eros, of more life.

Ascent, Immersion, Narration

Robert B. Stepto

As I have suggested in previous chapters, the Afro-American pregeneric myth of the quest for freedom and literacy has occasioned two basic types of narrative expressions, the narratives of ascent and immersion. The classic ascent narrative launches an "enslaved" and semiliterate figure on a ritualized journey to a symbolic North; that journey is charted through spatial expressions of social structure, invariably systems of signs that the questing figure must read in order to be both increasingly literate and increasingly free. The ascent narrative conventionally ends with the questing figure situated in the least oppressive social structure afforded by the world of the narrative, and free in the sense that he or she has gained sufficient literacy to assume the mantle of an articulate survivor. As the phrase "articulate survivor" suggests, the hero or heroine of an ascent narrative must be willing to forsake familial or communal postures in the narrative's most oppressive social structure for a new posture in the least oppressive environment—at best, one of solitude; at worst, one of alienation. This last feature of the ascent narrative unquestionably helps bring about the rise and development of an immersion narrative in the tradition, for the immersion narrative is fundamentally an expression of a ritualized journey into a symbolic South, in which the protagonist seeks those aspects of tribal literacy that ameliorate, if not obliterate, the conditions imposed by solitude. The conventional immersion narrative ends almost paradoxically, with the questing figure located in or near the narrative's most oppressive social

From *From Behind the Veil: A Study of Afro-American Narrative.* © 1979 by the Board of Trustees of the University of Illinois. University of Illinois Press, 1979.

structure but free in the sense that he has gained or regained sufficient tribal literacy to assume the mantle of an articulate kinsman. As the phrase "articulate kinsman" suggests, the hero or heroine of an immersion narrative must be willing to forsake highly individualized mobility in the narrative's least oppressive social structure for a posture of relative stasis in the most oppressive environment, a loss that is only occasionally assuaged by the newfound balms of group identity. (The argument is, of course, that these "shared epiphanies" were previously unavailable to the questing figure when he or she was adrift in a state of solitude.) . . .

Before *Invisible Man,* Zora Neale Hurston's *Their Eyes Were Watching God* is quite likely the only truly coherent narrative of both ascent and immersion, primarily because her effort to create a particular kind of questing *heroine* liberates her from the task (the compulsion, perhaps) of revoicing many of the traditional tropes of ascent and immersion. Of course, Hurston's narrative is neither entirely new nor entirely "feminine." The house "full ah thoughts" to which Janie ascends after her ritualized journey of immersion with Tea Cake into the "muck" of the Everglades (recall here Du Bois's swamp in both *The Souls* and *The Quest of the Silver Fleece)* is clearly a private ritual ground, akin in construction if not in accoutrement to Du Bois's study. And Janie's posture as a storyteller—as an articulate figure knowledgeable of tribal tropes, (a feature probably overdone in the frame, but not the tale, of *Their Eyes)* and in apparent control of her personal history—is a familiar and valued final siting for a primary voice in an Afro-American narrative. Still, there is much that is new in *Their Eyes.* The narrative takes place in a seemingly ahistorical world: the spanking new all-black town is meticulously bereft of former slave cabins; there are no railroad trains, above or underground, with or without Jim Crow cars; Matt's mule is a bond with and catalyst for distinct tribal memories and rituals, but these do not include the hollow slogan, "forty acres and a mule"; Janie seeks freedom, selfhood, voice, and "living" but is hardly guided— or haunted—by Sojourner Truth or Harriet Tubman, let alone Frederick Douglass. But that world is actually a fresh expression of a history of assault. The first two men in Janie's adult life (Logan Killicks and Jody Starks) and the spatial configurations through which they define themselves and seek to impose definition upon Janie (notably, a rural and agrarian space on one hand and a somewhat urban and mercantile space on the other) provide as much social structure as the narrative requires. Furthermore, the narrative's frame—the conversation "in the present" between Janie and Pheoby—creates something new in that it, and not the tale, is Hurston's vehicle for presenting the communal and possibly archetypal aspects of Janie's quest and final posture. Presentation does not always provide substantiation, and the clanking of Hurston's narrative and rhetorical machinery calls attention to itself when Pheoby offers her sole remark in the final half of the frame: "Lawd! . . . Ah done growed ten feet higher from jus' listenin' tuh you, Janie. Ah ain't satisfied wid mahself no mo'. Ah means tuh make Sam take me fishin' wid him after this. Nobody better not criticize yuh in mah hearin'." But these minor imperfections do not delimit the narrative's grand effort to demystify and site the somewhat ethereal concept of group- and self-consciousness, forwarded especially by *The Souls of Black Folk* and *Cane*. Clearly, Hurston is after a treatment of Janie and Pheoby that releases them from their immediate posture of storyteller and listener, and that propels them to one in which their sisterhood suggests a special kinship among womankind at large.

The one great flaw in *Their Eyes* involves not the framing dialogue, but Janie's tale itself. Through the frame Hurston creates the essential illusion that Janie has achieved her voice (along with everything else), and that she has even wrested from menfolk some control of the tribal posture of the storyteller. But the tale undercuts much of this, not because of its content—indeed, episodes such as the one in which Janie verbally abuses Jody in public abets Hurston's strategy—but because of its narration. Hurston's curious insistence on having Janie's tale—her personal history in and as a literary form—told by an omniscent third person, rather than by a first-person narrator, implies that Janie has not really won her voice and self after all—that her author (who is, quite likely, the omniscient narrating voice) cannot see her way clear to giving Janie her voice outright. Here, I think, Hurston is genuinely caught in the dilemma of how she might both govern and exploit the autobiographical impulses that partially direct her creation of Janie. On one hand, third-person narration of Janie's tale helps to build a space (or at least the illusion of a space) between author and character, for the author and her audience alike; on the other, when told in this fashion control of the tale remains, no matter how unintended, with the author alone.

Despite this problem, *Their Eyes* is a seminal narrative in Afro-American letters. It forwards the historical consciousness of the tradition's narrative forms, and helps to define those kinds of narratives which will also advance the literature in their turn. The narrative successes and failures of *Their Eyes* effectively prefigure several types of narratives; but, given the problems I have just discussed, one might say that the example of *Their Eyes* calls for a narrative in which the primary figure (like Janie) achieves a space beyond those defined by the tropes of ascent and immersion, but (*unlike* Janie) also achieves authorial control over both the frame and tale of his or her personal history. In short, *Their Eyes,* as a narrative strategy in a continuum of narrative strategies, directs us most immediately to Ralph Ellison's *Invisible Man.* Janie is quite possibly more of a blood relative to Ellison's narrator than either the "male chauvinist" or "feminist" readers of the tradition would care to contemplate.

"This Infinity of Conscious Pain": Zora Neale Hurston and the Black Female Literary Tradition

Lorraine Bethel

Black women writers have consistently rejected the falsification of their Black female experience, thereby avoiding the negative stereotypes such falsification has often created in the white American female and Black male literary traditions. Unlike many of their Black male and white female peers, Black women writers have usually refused to dispense with whatever was clearly Black and/or female in their sensibilities in an effort to achieve the mythical "neutral" voice of universal art. Zora Neale Hurston's work, particularly the novel *Their Eyes Were Watching God,* exemplifies the immense potential contained in the Black female literary tradition for the resolution of critical aesthetic and political problems common to both the Afro-American and the American female literary traditions. Foremost among these problems is the question of how Black/female writers can create a body of literature capable of capturing the political and cultural realities of their experience while using literary forms created by and for white, upper-class men.

Hurston was a novelist, folklorist, and anthropologist. She was born in the all-Black town of Eatonville, Florida, around the turn of the century (there are conflicting theories about her exact birthdate). Always a rebellious, inquisitive child, she left home at the age of fourteen, when her mother died, and became a maid. She eventually worked as a wardrobe

From *All the Women Are White, All the Blacks Are Men, But Some of Us Are Brave: Black Women's Studies,* edited by Gloria T. Hull, Patricia Bell Scott, and Barbara Smith. © 1982 by the Feminist Press, Gloria T. Hull, Patricia Bell Scott and Barbara Smith.

maid for an actress—a major educational experience which gave Hurston the determination to attend school. She left the theatrical company to take evening classes in Maryland, and then went on to Morgan Academy in 1917.

Hurston did well in her courses and finished two years of work in one, graduating in 1918. She enrolled at Howard University and held part-time jobs as a manicurist, maid, and waitress to support herself until she graduated in 1920. She worked all the time but was always in debt—a situation that would continue until she died penniless in 1960. When she was at Howard, Hurston published her first literary work—a short story—and thus began a thirty-year career, publishing more fiction than any black American woman before her.

A large and important part of Hurston's career took place during the Harlem Renaissance, which began in the twenties while she was attending Howard. Hurston's best work, especially her novel *Their Eyes*, is the product of a Black female folk aesthetic and cultural sensibility that emerged from the best revolutionary ideals of the period. It also anticipates the comparable renaissance in contemporary women's literature. Despite, or perhaps because of, these achievements, Hurston, like many Black women writers, has suffered "intellectual lynching" at the hands of white and Black men and white women.

Typical of such treatment is the Black male critic Darwin Turner's description of Hurston's work as "artful, coy, irrational, superficial and shallow." As Barbara Smith observes, these remarks "bear no relationship to the actual quality of Hurston's achievements and result from the fact that Turner is completely insensitive to the sexual political dynamics of Hurston's life and writing."

I have subtitled this essay "Zora Neale Hurston and the Black Female Literary Tradition" because as a Black feminist critic I believe that there is a separable and identifiable tradition of Black women writers, simultaneously existing within and independent of the American, Afro-American, and American female literary traditions. Hurston's work forms a major part of this tradition and illustrates its unique simultaneity. The sheer volume of her work would make Hurston a central figure in Black female literature: she published three folklore collections, an autobiography, four novels, and various pieces of short fiction and articles, aside from accumulating a large body of unpublished work that includes several plays.

In order to present fully the dimensions of Hurston's achievements and to place them in their proper context, I will attempt here to outline briefly the principles involved both in the concept of a Black female literary tradition and in the black feminist critical perspective necessary to understand Hurston's life and work. Such a survey simplifies this tradition, but is adequate for our purpose.

Black feminist literary criticism offers a framework for identifying the common socio-esthetic problems of authors who attempt to fashion a literature of cultural identity in the midst of racial/sexual oppression. It incorporates a political analysis that enables us to comprehend and appreciate the incredible achievements Black women like Zora Neale Hurston make in establishing artistic and literary traditions of any sort, and to understand their qualities and sensibilities. Such understanding requires a consciousness of the oppression these artists faced daily in a society full of institutionalized and violent hatred for both their Black skins and their female bodies. Developing and maintaining this consciousness is a basic tenet of Black feminism.

Black women embody by their sheer physical presence two of the most hated identities in this racist/sexist country. Whiteness and maleness in this culture have been not only seen as physical identities, but codified into states of being and world views. The codification of Blackness and femaleness by whites and males is contained in the terms "thinking like a woman" and "acting like a nigger," both based on the premise that there are typically negative Black and female ways of acting and thinking. Therefore, the most pejorative concept in the white/male world view would be thinking and acting like a "nigger woman." This is useful for understanding literary criticism of Hurston's works, which often attacks her personally for simply conducting herself as what she was: a Black woman.

Black people have always bonded together in order to establish and maintain positive definitions of Blackness. The most important and common form of this racial bonding has been Afro-American folk culture: the musical, oral, and visual artistic expressions of Black identity that have been handed down from generation to generation. The Harlem Renaissance, whose spirit Hurston's work reflects, was a manifestation of this bonding, although it had many false revolutionaries and failed in some respects to realize its radical potential.

Yet, to see Hurston as simply Black-identified is not enough. Hurston wrote as a Black woman about her own experiences and therefore, in some respects, spoke to the general Black female experience in America. She wrote as a Black woman–identifed Black woman, valuing her experiences as a woman as well as a Black person in a society where these areas of experience are generally regarded as valueless, insignificant, and inferior to white/male culture.

Women in this country have defied the dominant sexist society by developing a type of folk culture and oral literature based on the use of gender solidarity and female bonding as self-affirming rituals. Black women have a long tradition of bonding together in a community that has been a source of survival information, and psychic and emotional support. We have a distinct Black woman–identified folk culture based on our experiences in this society: symbols, language, and modes of expression that specifically reflect the realities of our lives as Black females in a dominant white/male culture. Because Black women rarely gained access to literary expression, this Black woman–identified bonding and folk culture have often gone unrecorded except through our individual lives and memories.

In her essay "In Search of Our Mothers' Gardens," Alice Walker has spoken perceptively of the way in which the material, economic, and political conditions of Black women's lives in a racist/sexist society have restricted their artistic expression. The classist politics of culture have been criticized by Paul Lauter:

> Often, working-class art does not, at least initially, take written form, for a variety of reasons ranging from the denial of literacy to working people to the problem of access to media. For these and other reasons it simply is not useful to approach working-class art only in terms of a set of discrete texts—still the dominant mode of literary study today. Gaining a more coherent view of working-class culture requires, we think, an effort to break out of such restrictive categories and to unify the study of the variety of forms—written poetry, oral poetry, needlework, for example—discussed here.

The holistic analysis Lauter proposes is also necessary to achieve a meaningful examination of Black women's culture.

Hurston's novel *Their Eyes* offers an excellent source for demonstrating the value of an interdisciplinary approach to Black women's culture in general and the Black female literary tradition in particular. Hurston locates her fiction firmly in Black women's traditional culture as developed and displayed through music and song. In presenting Janie's story as a narrative related by herself to her best Black woman friend, Pheoby, Hurston is able to draw upon the rich oral legacy of Black female storytelling and myth-making that has its roots in Afro-American culture. The reader who is conscious of this tradition will experience the novel as an overheard conversation as well as a literary text.

Janie's narrative in *Their Eyes* reflects the Black female blues esthetic—

the very direct use to which Black Women put language and song, in order, as critic Joanne Braxton states, to "transcend the most brutal, painful and personal of disasters in daily life and go on fighting—strong and alive." The blues, according to Ralph Ellison, "does not skirt the painful facts of human experience, but works through them to an artistic transcendence"; Gene Bluestein relates this to "the formula of Emerson's prescription for achieving the epiphanic moment—to work through the natural fact in order to express the spiritual truth that underlies it." Similarly, Janie, in her epiphanic experience with a blossoming pear tree, works through the physical and natural phenomena surrounding her in order to understand and express their underlying spiritual truths. As soon as Janie is able to formulate a vision of lyric selfhood, she must confront the obstacles that would prevent her from achieving it.

These obstacles are conveyed in *Their Eyes* partially through Hurston's use of symbolic geography. Janie's lyric vision is conceived outdoors, in her grandmother's "garden field." When Janie goes inside the house, she reaches "the narrow hallway" and remembers that her grandmother is "home with a sick headache." As soon as she is outside, Janie asks herself where the "singing bees" of her lyric vision are, and we are told that "nothing on the place nor in her grandma's house answered her. She searched as much of the world as she could from the top of the front steps and then went on down to the front gate and leaned over to gaze up and down the road. Looking, waiting, breathing short with impatience. Waiting for the world to be made."

A sense of the confinement and limitations of Janie's life with her grandmother comes through clearly in this passage. The small part of the world that Janie is able to observe from her grandmother's house is juxtaposed against the vast possibilities presented by the open road. Hurston is striving here to create symbols, images, and metaphors that can express Black female culture and experience. The metaphor of the open road comes in the first of a series of episodes in which Janie moves from the confinement of inner spaces into the open and down the road in search of her vision. Janie's search for answers to the questions posed by her lyric vision leads her to kiss Johnny Taylor. Both she and her grandmother experience the incident in a dreamlike state, but Janie's is induced by the intoxicating spring, while Nanny's comes from her illness and old age.

Hurston's first description of Nanny in *Their Eyes* establishes her as a representative of the religious experience that stands at the center of the Afro-American folk tradition. She is described in terms suggestive of a Christ figure. Janie makes Nanny a wreath of "palma christi leaves," and the words "bore" and "pierce" used in this passage invoke images of the crucifixion. While Janie represents the Black female folk aesthetic contained in the blues, her grandmother symbolizes the Black religious folk tradition embodied by spirituals.

The symbolic functions of Janie and Nanny are further established by their confrontation concerning Johnny Taylor's kiss. Nanny insists that Janie must get married immediately. Although she recognizes the innocence in Janie's action, Nanny is also acutely aware of the painful realities that make such exploration a luxury Janie cannot afford. Males like Johnny Taylor will perceive her now as sexually mature and an appropriate target for their advances. Her womanhood is forced upon her while she is still a child of sixteen because she is a Black female. Janie fails to understand this, however, and when she stubbornly rejects Nanny's suggestion that she marry Logan Killicks, a middle-aged widower, her grandmother slaps her.

Nanny's violent reaction to Janie's impulse to individuality is a protective measure like those defined by Ellison as characteristic of the southern Black community. She is attempting to adjust Janie to the prevailing sexual and racial milieu, and her protectiveness emerges as violence directed against Janie. Nanny attempts to explain to Janie the historical and social forces that make her innocent actions so serious:

> "Honey, de white man is de ruler of everything as fur as Ah been able tuh find out. Maybe it's some place way off in de ocean where de black man is in power, but we don't know nothin' but what we see. So de white man throw down de load and tell de nigger man tuh pick it up. He pick it up because he have to, but he don't tote it. He hand it to his women-folks. *De nigger woman is de mule uh de world so fur as Ah can see.* Ah been prayin' for it tuh be different wid you. Lawd, Lawd, Lawd!"

Throughout the remainder of the novel we observe Janie's struggle against conforming to this definition of the Black woman as "de mule uh de world." Its cruelty stands out starkly against the potential contained in Janie's youthful vision. The image of Janie and Nanny as victims of oppressive forces neither of them can alter is powerful and moving. We are led to think of countless Black females coming of age, and countless Black grandmothers and mothers confronting them with the harsh realities of Black women's lives in a racist, sexist society. In this sense Janie and her grandmother illustrate the tragic continuity of Black female oppression in white/male America.

Because this oppression has assumed different forms in their lives, Janie and Nanny have developed conflicting world views. Janie is experiencing a need to explore the answers to the life questions symbolized by her lyric encounter with the pear tree. She can only see marriage to Killicks as an obstacle to such explorations, yet she cannot communicate the reality of her lyric vision to her grandmother, whose sensibilities are restricted by her nearness to the slave experience. Nanny reveals her proximity to this experience when she tells her slave narrative while "rocking Janie like an infant." Nanny's tale of sexual abuse and violence contrasts starkly with Janie's innocence, and makes the premature ending of her childhood seem all the more tragic.

Nanny relates that she was raped by her master, and that after he left for the war, she was subjected to physical abuse by his wife. While recovering from childbirth, she was forced to escape with her week-old child. Nanny's desires to do something in praise of Black women, frustrated by sexual exploitation and slavery, were transferred to her daughter, Leafy, whom she prepared for a career as a teacher. This dream was also destroyed by particularly cruel and ironic sexual violence when the schoolteacher raped Leafy in the woods where Nanny had hidden to escape to freedom.

By the time of Janie's coming of age, Nanny's aspirations have been modified by the violent realities of Black female life in American society. Her horrible experiences have led her to see the domestic pedestal as the safest escape from the dangers of racial/sexual oppression. As Killicks's wife Janie will be assured that "no trashy nigger, no breath-and-britches, lak Johnny Taylor," will use her "body to wipe his foots on," and that no "menfolks white or black" will make "a spit cup outa" her. As Smith states, "Hurston is fully aware of the fundamental oppressiveness of traditional marriage, yet she has a deep understanding of what the institution represents to women who were formerly enslaved."

Janie complies with her grandmother's request. She replaces her search for identity, as symbolized by the pear tree, with a search for romantic love in marriage. The remainder of *Their Eyes* details the shattering of Janie's romantic illusions as she becomes conscious of the tyranny of the pedestal her grandmother chose for her. Only after this process is completed does it become possible for Janie to once again become a Black woman in search of herself.

Hurston satirizes the romantic ideals that Janie uses to make "a sort of comfort for herself" when she marries Killicks. When Janie goes inside Killicks's house "to wait for love to begin," she is both a tragic and a comic figure. Eventually she begins to suspect that love does not come automatically with marriage and confronts her grandmother with the discrepancy:

"You told me Ah mus gointer love him, and Ah don't. Maybe if somebody was to tell me how, Ah could do it." Nanny's reaction reveals her familiarity with the unpleasant realities of married life for women. Her first thoughts are that Janie is pregnant, or that Logan has been abusing her: "Don't tell me you done got knocked up already, less see—dis Saturday it's two months and two weeks. . . . You and Logan been fussin'? Lawd, Ah know dat grass-gut liver-lipted nigger ain't done took and beat mah baby already." The "already" in both sentences indicates that Nanny views pregnancy and violence as inevitable companions of married life for women. Her familiarity with domestic and sexual violence is also revealed when she explains to Janie earlier her reason for remaining unmarried once slavery ended: "Ah wouldn't marry nobody, though Ah could have uh heap uh times, cause Ah didn't want nobody mistreating mah baby."

Janie is still unable to communicate to Nanny the substance of the ideals symbolized by the pear tree. Though she sympathizes with her grand-daughter, Nanny remains convinced that marriage to Killicks is the best possible arrangement for Janie. Nanny's religious beliefs to some extent allow her to justify Janie's suffering with the principle that "folks is meant to cry 'bout somethin' or other." Her character also reflects the solemnity and dignity inherent in the Afro-American female folk religious tradition and sensibility:

> Nanny sent Janie along with a stern mien, but she dwindled all the rest of the day as she worked. And when she gained the privacy of her own little shack she stayed on her knees so long she forgot she was there herself. There is a basin in the mind where words float around on thought and thought on sound and sight. Then there is a depth of thought untouched by words, and deeper still a gulf of formless feelings untouched by thought. Nanny entered this infinity of conscious pain again on her old knees. Towards morning she muttered, "Lawd, you know mah heart. Ah done de best Ah could do. De rest is left to you." She scuffled up from her knees and fell heavily across the bed. A month later she was dead.

The "infinity of conscious pain" involved in the dynamics of Black womanhood in America was a permanent reality for Zora Neale Hurston. She not only had to deal with the racial/sexual politics of day-to-day life as a Black woman, but she chose to confront life as an independent, woman-identified Black female artist and social scientist, a stance requiring great courage and strength.

Black woman identification, the basis of Black feminism and Black feminist literary criticism, is most simply the idea of Black women seeking their own identity and defining themselves through bonding on various levels—psychic, intellectual, and emotional, as well as physical—with other Black women. Choosing Black lesbianism, feminism, or woman-identification is the political process and struggle of choosing a hated identity: choosing to be a Black woman, not only in body, but in spirit as well. It is the process of identifying one's self and the selves of other Black women as inherently valuable, and it is perceived by the dominant white/male culture as most threatening because it challenges that culture's foundations. Black woman identification is Black women not accepting male—including Black male—definitions of femaleness or Black womanhood, just as Black identification consists of Blacks rejecting white definitions of Blackness and creating autonomous standards for evaluating Black culture.

"Tuh de Horizon and Back": The Female Quest in *Their Eyes Were Watching God*

Missy Dehn Kubitschek

The common critical portrait of Zora Neale Hurston is that of a romantic elitist separated from the day-to-day life of most of her black contemporaries. In the context of this picture, *Their Eyes Were Watching God* provides an emblem of Hurston's withdrawal from political concerns in favor of personal relationships. Originating in Hurston's abrasive personality and in the first readings of her work, this view has become the premise supporting—and reinforced by—sexist assumptions concerning Janie, her heroine of *Their Eyes Were Watching God*. These assumptions obscure Janie's role as the heroine of a successful quest and reinforce the distortion of Hurston's view of the black artist's relationship to his or her community. In fact, Janie, always sufficiently knowledgeable of white culture to ensure her survival, discovers her own soul only through the art of storytelling, thus intimating the artist's responsibility to, and dependence on, the larger community. *Their Eyes Were Watching God* does not portray the artist as an individual of superior sensitivity who comes equipped with a portable pedestal, but as a middle-aged, blue-jeaned woman talking with neighbors. Concentrating on the individual quest which secures the boon, the novel strongly implies communal enjoyment of, and benefit from, the quester's prize.

The quest motif structures the entire novel: Janie twice leaves established social positions for a more adventurous life, descends into the underworld of the hurricane, faces a literal trial following Tea Cake's death,

From *Black American Literature Forum* 17, no. 3 (Fall 1983). © 1983 by Indiana State University.

and returns to Eatonville with her hard-won knowledge. Given this structure, the pervasive critical silence on the issue raises important questions concerning the biases conditioning discussion of *Their Eyes*. Of the numerous commentators, only Sherley Anne Williams and Robert Stepto treat Janie as a questing heroine or suggest her journey's archetypal significance.

Indeed, only very lately have critics allowed Janie to be the heroine of her own story, much less the successful quester returning with a boon for her community. Attacking the tradition of such limiting criticism as "intellectual lynching," Mary Helen Washington has led the way in reasserting the centrality of Janie's search for identity and her connections to her community.

With these exceptions, the critical consensus condescends to and oversimplifies Hurston's art and Janie's experience. Darwin Turner's portrait of Janie typifies this consensus: "All Janie wants is to love, to be loved, and to share the life of her man. But, like the witch in the Wife of Bath's tale, she first must find a man wise enough to let her be whatever kind of woman she wants to be." Turner's statement, with its strong bias concerning the place of romantic love in the heroine's life, carries on a venerable tradition of oversimplification of women authors. In tone and sensibility it resembles William Makepeace Thackeray's discussion of Charlotte Brontë's *Villette:* "it amuses me to read the author's naïve confession of being in love with 2 men at the same time; and her readiness to fall in love at any time. The poor little woman of genius! the fiery little eager brave tremulous home-faced creature! . . . rather than have fame, rather than any other earthly good or mayhap heavenly one she wants some Tomkins or another to love her and be in love with." Although Turner does not in this passage follow his attack from character to author, the similarity of these two commentaries is striking and profoundly disturbing. Underestimating Hurston's artistry, Turner addresses only Janie's narration, overlooking the frame story of her continuing relationship with Eatonville and with Pheoby, which is central to the quest motif. Turner's perceptions contain kernels of truth: Love *does* compose an essential element of Janie's—and Hurston's—vision. But neither that love nor that vision remains simple. Her guiding image of the pear tree in bloom bespeaks a more profound meaning for love than Turner's passage implies. Sexuality does not simply bind Janie to an individual man. Human life and love develop within the cycle of the seasons, assuming not only domestic and social but also a natural and transcendent meaning. In fact, to attain this transcendence, Janie and Tea Cake must completely reconstruct their domestic roles. Their challenge of the whole social structure renders Turner's focus on private, romantic love untenable. The novel's very title, referring to human awe and loss of ego in the face of overwhelming power, directs us to a wider, archetypal focus.

Very few critics, however, recognize in Janie the independence and strength of the archetypal quester. Rather, they diminish her, denying her an independent sphere of action and being. James R. Giles, for example, sees other characters as representatives of contending forces but views Janie only as a passive prize: "The major underlying theme is contained in the contrast between those characters (Nannie [sic] and Jody, especially) who are so white-oriented that they measure time in a rational, materialistic way and those whose blackness is so intact that they view time emotionally and hedonistically (Tea-Cake [sic], primarily). It is for the dominance of Janie's soul that they struggle; and Tea-Cake [sic] or black purity, wins. Giles's opposition between black and white systems is clearly accurate; his extension of the issue to time is at least tenable; and his last statement is indefensibly sexist. He reduces Janie to a counter, fought over and finally claimed by external forces. Far from remaining passive, Janie struggles with issues in order to bring her own life into harmony with her original vision of the pear tree. Only a manifestation of natural power, the hurricane, ever dominates Janie. Her soul remains triumphantly her own.

Even critics alert to sexism tend to subordinate Janie. S. Jay Walker's "Zora Neale Hurston's *Their Eyes Were Watching God*: Black Novel of Sexism" occasionally slips in ways which have far-reaching implications. Walker notes, for instance, that the novel "is something less than a primer of romanticized love. At one point, Tea Cake, jealous of a suspected rival, beats Janie; at another, Janie, having the same suspicion, beats Tea Cake." By reversing the order of the events, probably unintentionally, Walker implies that Janie's action is derivative of Tea Cake's, supporting the tendency to see Tea Cake as a dominating force. Other less perceptive critics reveal the dangers inherent in this tendency when they present Tea Cake as the dominant male lover whom they see as central to Hurston's vision.

Perceiving Janie as a derivative personality, these critics remain blind to her courage in exploring uncharted psychic territory and communicating her discoveries to others. Having defined the heroine as incapable of sustaining a quest, they are forced to look to another character for true heroism. Marion Kilson demonstrates this redefinition in its clearest form: "A second recurrent theme in Hurston's fiction was the purposeful, self-reliant, industrious, and courageous wanderer as an ideal male type. He appeared as Tea Cake in *Their Eyes Were Watching God*, Moses in *Moses*, and Jim Meserve in *Seraph on the Suwanee*. Theoretically he was complemented by the ideal woman, his strong supportive spouse who could assume an independent and self-reliant role herself if the situation required it." Tea Cake industrious? Janie a complement? Although *Moses* is named for its protagonist, *Their Eyes* is not named for Tea Cake, who enters halfway through the novel. *Their Eyes Were Watching God* focuses on Janie and her community, of which Tea Cake is only one important member. Detailing her quest for self-discovery and self-definition, it celebrates her as an artist who enriches Eatonville by communicating her understanding.

Janie attains this understanding by carrying out a successful quest, such as that defined by Joseph Campbell in *The Hero With a Thousand Faces*. Campbell delineates several components of the quest: answering the call to adventure, crossing the threshold into the unknown, facing various trials, finding the reward (either concrete or symbolic), and returning to the community. Campbell emphasizes the flexibility of this pattern, parts of which may be truncated or even absent to allow greater development of others. The first half of *Their Eyes* deals with Janie's initial refusal to answer the call to adventure; the second details her trials; the all-but-overlooked and crucial frame story concerns her return to community and the resultant possibility for communal as well as personal growth.

The call to adventure comes through Janie's vision of the pear tree being pollinated by bees. In this vision, a real pear tree in Nanny's yard acquires transcendent significance. When Janie perceives a bee penetrating a blossom of this tree, she vicariously experiences that sexuality and thinks "so this was a marriage!" This identification of marriage with total fulfillment, however, reflects her immature consciousness. Critics limiting their focus to romantic love fail to recognize that the mature Janie reimagines the tree in a way which deepens its resonance. The middle-aged Janie, preparing to tell her story to Pheoby, "saw her life like a great tree in leaf with the things suffered, things enjoyed, things done and undone. Dawn and doom was in the branches." Clearly, the tree symbolizes human life, and the seasonal change in the tree, which is now in leaf rather than in bloom, corresponds to Janie's time of life. Her initial interpretation of the tree is essentially static, focused on the social institution of marriage. Her later, more sophisticated vision centers on the balance of opposites, "things done and undone" (perhaps even the union of opposites, since the singlar verb "was" indicates a singular subject in "dawn and doom"). Through her quest, Janie attempts to harmonize her daily life with her ideal image derived from the pear tree. When she returns to Eatonville and recounts her adventures to Pheoby, Janie senses no dissonance between her experience and her vision. But to achieve that fulfillment, she must struggle through many years when the image remains tantalizing but seemingly unrealizable.

This divorce of Janie's life from her vision of fulfillment results from her initial refusal of the call to adventure. Her temporizing stems in part from the pressures exerted by her grandmother, pressures reinforced by her geographic and psychic isolation. Indeed, the responsibility for her unfulfilling marriage, contracted when she is only sixteen, lies largely with these forces. Aware that Logan Killicks has nothing to do with the pear tree, she is led to believe, particularly by Nanny, that no matter who the marriage partner, a congruence between the image and the reality will develop gradually. Her hope of developing harmony between her marriage and the pear tree evaporates when Logan refuses to accept essential parts of her heritage, personality, and experience. As soon as she discovers that Logan "was accusing her of her mama, her grandmama and her feelings, and she couldn't do anything about any of it," she jettisons her commitment to him and seeks adventure with Jody Starks.

At this point, however, Janie cannot conceptualize a true quest capable of uniting the quotidian and the transcendent. At the outset, she knows that Jody is not himself a part of the pear tree vision, that "he did not represent sun-up and pollen and blooming trees, but he spoke for far horizon." A short time later, however, she seeks to realize her vision by disguising the concrete reality which should embody it: "From now on until death she was going to have flower dust and springtime sprinkled over everything. A bee for her bloom." Janie no longer sees Jody as a vehicle but as the thing-in-itself. When she cannot sustain the fiction, she consciously decides to live in bad faith: " 'Maybe he ain't nothin',' she cautioned herself, 'but he is something in my mouth. He's got tuh be else Ah ain't got nothin' tuh live for. Ah'll lie and say he is. If Ah don't, life won't be nothin' but uh store and uh house.' " Janie bears complete responsibility for her own unhappiness in this marriage. Given the natures of Janie and Jody, the marriage could never have succeeded. But Janie here temporizes as she did not when confronted with Logan's intractability. Her failure of courage and imagination results in an insistence both public and private that the marriage is a success. The price of this bad faith is almost twenty years of spiritual hibernation, complete separation of concrete reality from the vision of the pear tree. She has temporarily refused the call to adventure in favor of a specious security.

As Nanny's death freed Janie from her first entrapment, so Jody's death frees her from her second retreat from the quest. Thereafter, Janie becomes an active agent in her own life; her acceptance of existential responsibility makes her truly, as opposed to nominally, free. Hurston underscores Janie's rebirth by associating her reflections on her marriages with a creation myth:

> She had found a jewel down inside herself and she had wanted to walk where people could see her and gleam it around. But she had been set in the market-place to sell. Been set for still-bait. When God had made The Man, he made him out of stuff that sung all the time and glittered all over. Then after that some angels got jealous and chopped him into millions of pieces, but still he glittered and hummed. So they beat him down to nothing but sparks but each little spark had a shine and a song. So they covered each one over with mud. And the lonesomeness in the sparks make them hunt for one another, but the mud is deaf and dumb. Like all the other tumbling mud-balls, Janie had tried to show her shine.

This irreverent, edited, and conflated variation of *Paradise Lost* and several Egyptian myths emphasizes both the mud and the shine. Previously Janie has been aware only of her shine. She must also accept the mud of the Everglades in order to realize fully her vision of the pear tree.

Before experiencing the community of the Everglades and Tea Cake's love, Janie must cross the threshold, separating specious safety from the risk necessary to fulfillment. She refuses offers of marriage, recognizing that their offers of "protection" amount to no more than economic exploitation. Her life alone, while it has no connection with the pear tree, has few uncertainties. Accepting Tea Cake's offer of companionship and love, on the other hand, carries tremendous risk. The community (represented by Hezekiah) warns Janie that Tea Cake will exploit her sexually and financially and then abandon her. Having internalized this concept, Janie nonetheless acts on her feeling with only Tea Cake's verbal reassurance. She cannot have an advance guarantee of his intentions; only his actions can certify his sincerity.

These actions are not initially encouraging. In Jacksonville, Tea Cake borrows Janie's money for a gambling stake without first consulting her. Alone for a day and a half with no word, Janie fears the fulfillment of the Eatonville prophecy that she will return home alone and broke. When Tea Cake returns and explains the reasons for his actions, and reaffirms his commitment to her, Janie fully accepts their relationship and its implicit call to adventure. She thus embarks on the quest to unify her life and its ideal image.

As part of this quest, Janie and Tea Cake undergo various trials and redefine their lives outside the usual social constructs. Their relationship rejects ordinary conceptions of dominant and subordinate sex roles. Tea Cake is Janie's companion on her quest, not her master or mentor. In the Jacksonville incident, for example, she asserts her right to full participation in community activity after Tea Cake has excluded her from his party, fearing that the "refined" Janie will be revolted. Tea Cake's action recalls Jody's prohibitions against Janie's participation in community affairs such as the wake for the mule or the storytelling sessions. Whereas Jody actively imposes a certain gentility on Janie, Tea Cake simply assumes its presence. As part of her determination to " 'utilize mahself all over,' " she insists that she be allowed to stand, not on a pedestal, but on the ground. This exploration of new roles continues in the Everglades, where Janie develops traditionally masculine skills such as marksmanship. Clearly, the adjustment involves more than Janie's expansion into previously male roles: Just as she works beside Tea Cake in the fields, he helps prepare supper. By abandoning traditional limitations, they approach the joyous harmony of Janie's vision.

Their lives are not, however, simply a continuous celebration. As questing heroine, Janie must face trials with their origins in individuals, society, and natural forces, Janie's first trial centers on Tea Cake and the possibility of personal betrayal. She insists that Tea Cake admit this possibility when she discovers him wrestling with Nunkie, obviously responding on some level to a sexual invitation. Significantly, Janie is so angry that she strikes Tea Cake, indicating her rejection of her earlier passivity. Previously, Janie has accepted blows from Nanny and Jody without physical reply. Here, rather than accepting an imposed will, she forces a confrontation on her own terms. (Later she will accept Tea Cake's right to express his anxieties over Mrs. Turner's brother in the same way.) Following this trial, she accepts Tea Cake's reaffirmation of his love, and there are no more wrestling matches. Nevertheless, she has learned that any real commitment must risk betrayal.

Janie has more preparation for the social trial represented by Mrs. Turner, a light-skinned black woman who idolizes white culture. Janie very early accepts her blackness (though she at first resists it when she sees a picture of herself with white children) and later rejects Nanny and Jody's unsatisfying white system. Not personally threatened by Mrs. Turner's self-hatred and racism, Janie fails at first to understand the depth of that threat to Tea Cake and the rest of the black community. She tolerates Mrs. Turner's presence even when Mrs. Turner criticizes Tea Cake and offers her light brother as a more socially desirable spouse. Janie limits her reproofs to mild hints and rudenesses which Mrs. Turner can rationalize as the prerogative of Janie's lighter skin. Still, Janie does not fail this trial, for she accepts Tea Cake's anger and does not interfere with the community's violent annihilation of this threat to its integrity.

The hurricane, a trial generated by nature, threatens physical survival just as individual and social betrayals threaten psychic survival. Those caught in the hurricane shed their social roles: "The time was past for asking the white folks what to look for through that door. Six eyes were questioning *God*." Under these circumstances, attempts to react to or protect another endanger oneself. When Janie tries to secure a shingle to shelter Tea Cake, it acts as a sail, and the hurricane blows her into the water; when Tea Cake sees her drowning, he rescues her at the cost of the fatal dog bite. An elemental and divine force, the hurricane reduces the personality to its essential, forces a confrontation with physical limits. If the celebratory life on the Everglades is the "dawn" in the branches of Janie's pear-tree vision, then the hurricane is certainly part of the "doom." Up to this point, Janie has not had to contemplate the death of anyone dear to her, much less her own mortality.

The experience of the hurricane not only creates the physical circumstances leading to Tea Cake's death, it raises the metaphysical issues involved in humanity's complex relationships with nature and death. Janie has recognized fate's power during Jody's illness, but while she pities him, she has much more emotional investment in Tea Cake, whose madness and death try her strength severely. Janie ultimately accepts memory as a means of transcending death, which she perceives as a part of the natural cycle. At the same time, she expresses an immediate grief and longing which that acceptance cannot obliterate: "No hour is ever eternity, but it has its right to weep." Transcendent vision must expand rather than deny the concrete reality if an individual is to live the integrated life which is the reward of the successful questing heroine.

Janie's reward is full participation in a process of community expression and construction, a process from which Nanny and Jody had previously isolated her. As Jody's wife, Janie can participate only in extremely circumscribed ways. She first feels an unpleasant restriction when Jody refuses to let her respond to an invitation to speak on their first night in Eatonville. Jody enforces this denial of Janie's voice by forbidding her to take part in either the storytelling activities of Eatonville or its "low-life" communal celebrations. Janie disguises her only public rebellion as praise of Jody. Even then, Janie's remark that " 'You got uh town so you freed uh mule' " passes without notice of its irony.

Her participation in the Everglades community contrasts dynamically with this restricted relationship to Eatonville, just as her partnership with Tea Cake contrasts with her subordination to Jody. Janie listens to lying contests and stories in Belle Glade, just as she did in Eatonville, but she begins to create and tell stories herself and, through practice, becomes good at it. These storytelling sessions are crucial to community unity and self-definition, since they generate and develop communal tradition. Participation in this process is also crucial for the individual's self-definition, since communal traditions define available roles. Janie's previous passivity, enforced by Jody and by her own avoidance of a confrontation with him, locks her into a fixed role: Her active participation in the storytelling on the Glades exemplifies Hurston's vision of the relationship between communal and individual definition.

Robert Hemenway succinctly describes Hurston's attitude toward this creative process: "Hurston alone, among all the artists of the Harlem Renaissance, understood this principle of folk *process*. Folk tradition is not just a body of texts, melodies, and beliefs. . . . Folk tradition involves *behavior*— performed interpretations of the world which influence action—and it does not easily transfer to a print-oriented tradition. . . . There is not separation of subject and object, of mind and material in folk tradition. What appears from afar as material for the creative artist is simply behavior for the tale-teller, an activity as natural as thinking; traditional art is perpetuated without self-consciousness." Hurston shows Janie's artistic temperament, previously limited to private and escapist images of the pear tree, now expressing itself in communal creation, integrating her concrete experience and her transcendent vision.

This integration, because it does not rest on denial of reality, actually encourages concrete changes. Janie and Tea Cake effect a substantial change in the community's definition of itself: "Since Tea Cake and Janie had friended with the Bahaman workers in the 'Glades, they, the 'Saws,' had been gradually drawn into the American crowd. They quit hiding out to hold their dances when they found that their American friends didn't laugh at them as they feared. Many of the Americans learned to jump and liked it as much as the 'Saws.' " Thus, the original community of Americans expands to include the Bahamans. Rather than demanding assimilation, it accepts and adopts the Bahamans' characteristic artistic expression.

For Janie, full participation in the life of her community must include observing, experiencing, and expressing violence. Earlier, Janie has been distanced from all but nominal violence. Nanny's desire to protect Janie from the violence which destroyed her mother motivates her insistence on the marriage to Logan. Later, Janie's position as Mrs. Mayor Starks insulates her from physical violence—except from Jody's hand. As an extension of emotional intensity, physical violence is a necessary component of Janie's desire to experience truly and fully: nature contains both the pear tree and the hurricane; communities have both celebrations and brawls; individuals have both compassion and more violent feelings. Despite attempts to distance her, violent feelings play a pervasive role in shaping Janie's experience. Violence twice precipitates a change in her life: Nanny's slaps help persuade Janie to marry Logan; Jody's slaps encourage her to separate her internal and external lives in order to survive. Janie reacts to this violence by some manner of accommodation; it does not occur to her to defend herself physically. Significantly, Janie battles Jody according to his own rules, so that her single victory is verbal. Janie's reaction to the cruel pursuit of the mule is in one sense a reaction to her own plight, for Nanny has identified the black woman as the mule of the world, and Janie protectively feels that "people ought to have some regard for helpless things." By the time that she and Tea Cake arrive in the Everglades, Janie no longer wants compassion or protection from violence. Admitting the depth and intensity of her feelings, she is willing to use physical violence to combat the threat of Nunkie. Similarly she accepts Tea Cake's violent protest over Mrs. Turner's brother without flinching, for these are not, like the earlier experiences, examples of violence used to enforce an action or behavior, but violence used to make another person aware.

Having experienced and accepted individual violence, Janie learns the potential of communal violence for self-defense. The possibility of violence in Belle Glade forces the police chief to allow the community its own forms of celebration on pay day: "Not enough jail-space for all the drunks so why bother with a few? All he could do to keep down fights and get the white men out of colored town by nine o'clock." This potential violence can become actual if necessary. When her family fails to control Mrs. Turner's potentially disruptive attitudes, for instance, the community expels them by an organized brawl in the business establishment. The very nature of Mrs. Turner's prejudices makes her impervious to milder warnings—only violence can protect the community. Janie protects herself in an analogous manner when she kills Tea Cake. Maddened by rabies, Tea Cake attacks Janie, intending to kill her. Since his disease destroys any possible awareness, Janie has no choice other than physical violence. Having experienced the violence in herself, in nature, and in the community, Janie returns to Eatonville to relate her story, fulfilling her function as revelatory artist.

The return of the questing hero to the original community is fraught with difficulties. Indeed, the inability of the hero to reintegrate self and community has been defined as characteristic of the American quest. Janie's attitude toward Eatonville on her return cannot easily be summed up; it says yes and says no in ways that reflect Hurston's ambivalence toward racial and communal definitions of her identity. On the one hand, Hurston resented her white patron's attempts to control her work as a folklorist and artist, and she insisted on the value of black art as represented in the folktales and spirituals. On the other hand, she resisted racial definitions of self, which she felt rested on stereotypes of victimized blacks, and thus infuriated those like Arna Bontemps, Richard Wright, and Alain Locke, who felt that her books simply ignored basic facts of Afro-American life. Janie shares both Hurston's aggressive desire to be free of social categorization and her contempt for the less adventurous; simply identifying Hurston's views with Janie's oversimplifies the novel, however. Hurston provides Janie with a suitable lover whom she herself never found, and Janie finds a genuine community (in Belle Glade) which Hurston never experienced, at least as an adult.

Even for the fictional character, full participation in a true community cannot make life idyllic, of course. Nevertheless, Janie values Belle Glade sufficiently to forgive its betrayal of her. When Janie stands trial for killing Tea Cake, the black community judges her guilty of murder, tries to testify against her, and objects to the white jurors' decison to acquit her. But Janie's grief for Tea Cake crowds out any resentment. In addition, as a real part of the community, Janie is able to fathom its motives and understands that it is acting from grief rather than malice. She forgives the ringleaders, who then participate in the funeral procession. To assure the community that she has forgiven it, she consents to remain in the Everglades for a few more weeks.

Janie is more aloof on her first evening back in Eatonville. Seemingly uninterested in participating fully in the Eatonville community, she expresses her ambivalences clearly to Pheoby:

> "Ah don't mean to bother wid tellin' 'em nothin', Pheoby. Tain't worth de trouble. You can tell 'em what Ah say if you wants to. Dat's just de same as me 'cause mah tongue is in mah friend's mouf."
>
> "If you so desire Ah'll tell 'em what you tell me to tell 'em."
>
> "To start off wid, people like dem wastes up too much time puttin' they mouf on things they don't know nothin' about."

Although Janie here denies interest in communicating with the rest of the community, she accepts Pheoby as her mouthpiece. Shortly thereafter, she describes both her potential audience and herself without such bitterness: " 'If they wants to see and know, why don't they come kiss and be kissed?' " (Later she describes her relationship with Pheoby as one between "kissin'-friends.") She continues: " 'Ah could then sit down and tell 'em things. Ah been a delegate to de big 'ssociation of life. Yessuh! De Grand Lodge, de big convention of livin' is just where Ah been dis year and a half y'all aint seen me.' " Janie's aloofness on returning to Eatonville reflects her recognition that it, like Belle Glade, must be allowed to judge the unfamiliar before it can hear the truth and revise the judgment. Having experienced adventures beyond the common ken of Eatonville, Janie is eager to speak, "full of that oldest human longing, self-revelation." The town's earlier willingness to hear Janie speak indicated that she will before long have an audience of more than Pheoby. The immediate effect upon Pheoby is that traditionally desired by returned questers, the expansion of consciousness represented by her statement that " 'Ah done growed ten feet higher from jus' listenin' tuh you, Janie. Ah ain't satisfied wid mahself no mo'.' " Janie cautions against simple-minded attempts to duplicate in detail her own adventures: " 'Pheoby, you got tuh *go* there tuh *know* there.' " Having been " 'tuh de horizon and back,' " she realizes the personal nature of the quest.

Though Walker and Stepto have commented on Janie's return to Eatonville no critic has yet explored her return to that particular community and her function as provocative storyteller. Why does she return at all, given that, despite her grief for Tea Cake, she has a community in Belle Glade? Why does she not return to the community where she had lived with Nanny and Logan? The answers lie in the relationships between white and black values in these three communities, answers which address Addison Gayle's political attack on *Their Eyes*. Gayle writes:

> After returning to the town from which her search for freedom began, she [Janie] remains an outsider and yet is not able to continue her rebellion beyond the immediate present. Like Teacake [sic], she, too, is dead to the realities of the world in which she lives. For though the white world remains more symbol than actuality for her, it is in actuality that it is oppressive. Thus, the questioning, restless spirit which led her to rebellion against the tradition that circumscribes her, due to race and sex, must lead her to challenge the equally restrictive patterns that deny physical freedom. This was the task of writers more talented and more angry than Miss Hurston.

In fact, Janie's exploration has secured her physical and spiritual freedom, and her subsequent daily life in Eatonville serves as a liberating example.

Each community in the novel—that of Nanny, Eatonville, and Belle Glade—contains a black character or a group of black characters who have internalized white values. Hurston judges these characters in relation to their reasons for allowing themselves to be co-opted and their effects on Janie. Nanny, the most sympathetic, adopts white values to ensure the survival of her granddaughter; her effect on Janie testifies to the lasting effect of slavery. Jody and Mrs. Turner enslave themselves and are judged more harshly. Though she threatens Tea Cake, Mrs. Turner is finally pitiable because her esteem for white skin forces her to reject part of herself. Jody never suffers as the others do, and he refuses to confront the suffering that he causes (even Nanny listens to Janie's complaints). Two of these representatives of white values attain no noteworthy status: Nanny dies without having achieved outstanding economic or social success, and Mrs. Turner is driven out. The greater power of the analogous character in Eatonville, however, is never directly challenged. Any diminution of Jody's control stems from Janie's public insult to his virility, rather than from a refusal of his values. Furthermore, Janie, like Nanny and Mrs. Turner, has promoted white values, albeit more passively. By allowing Jody to control her, to place her on the pedestal without public protest, she has encouraged those like Pheoby to envy and emulate her. Gayle notwithstanding, Janie can and does continue her rebellion beyond the immediate present. She must exorcise her own earlier influence through storytelling and expiating example, through full participation in her community. Leaving in silk and returning in overalls is the first step; telling Pheoby her story, the second; living in her community, the third. Janie will continue to speak and act as a black woman artist in Eatonville, a position which places her in a unique position in regard to the Afro-American literary tradition.

In *From Behind the Veil*, Robert Stepto calls *Their Eyes Were Watching God* "quite likely the only truly coherent narrative of both ascent and immersion." Stepto's term "narrative of ascent" refers to a story in which the hero moves from a symbolic South of slavery to a less constraining symbolic North, attaining a literacy which refers to knowledge of the white-dominated society as well as reading and writing. The hero thus becomes an "articulate survivor" who pays for his/her triumph by becoming isolated from his/her original community. The "narrative of immersion," on the other hand, focuses on an "articulate kinsman" who moves from a symbolic North to a symbolic South, attaining "tribal literacy" and reintegration with the original community.

Certainly Stepto is right in seeing both types of narrative in *Their Eyes*. Janie begins articulate; her playmates nickname her "Alphabet," and growing up in the white folks' yard assures her literacy. Still, the nickname comes into existence because " 'so many people had done named me different names,' " and Janie doesn't realize that she's black until she sees a photograph of herself and her friends. Janie feels the isolation of the articulate survivor when she describes Nanny's philosophy and her own compliance with it: " 'She was borned in slavery time when folks, dat is black folks, didn't sit down anytime dey felt lak it. So sittin' on porches lak de white madam looked lak uh mighty fine thing tuh her. Dat's whut she wanted for me—don't keer whut it cost. Git up on uh high chair and sit dere. She didn't have time tuh think whut tuh do after you got up on de stool uh do nothin'. De object wuz tuh git dere. So Ah got up on de high stool lak she told me, but Pheoby, Ah done nearly languished tuh death up dere.' " Her ascent (what Hemenway calls Hurston's "vertical metaphor") alienates her from her communal roots and delays her response to the call to adventure. Janie discovers her real self only through immersion in the community of the Everglades, where she completes the patterns of ascent and immersion. By emphasizing the frame story and the pattern of the quest, Hurston extends the narrative pattern to include the effects of the heroine's ascent and immersion on the community. Janie becomes an articulate kinsman; she influences her first audience (Pheoby) and has reason to anticipate an expanded audience and extended effects for her art.

Their Eyes Were Watching God, then, intimates a third narrative, this time of group ascent. Group ascent would involve a community's growth to literacy and awareness of the modes of expression in surrounding white culture; its result, a literate community, would lessen or abolish the isolation of the individual articulate survivor. Although Jody's idea of establishing a post office in all-black Eatonville has the potential to aid in a group ascent, he can never successfully lead or join such a movement. Jody establishes a division between himself and the group—hence his emphasis on behavior appropriate for Mrs. Mayor Starks. Almost aspiring to the alienation which plagues Stepto's articulate survivor, the authoritarian Jody can never join, he can only command. The community accepts his material innovations, but, significantly, his assertion of superiority creates the isolation which makes his death so painful. With his position resting on the imposition of his "progressive" ideas rather than on a consensus reached through many individual contributions, Jody remains a superior rather than a leader among equals.

Amiri Baraka has described the tradition of leadership in the Afro-

American community in terms of a call-and-response pattern, analogous to that of work songs composed during slavery. In this pattern, a leader's call invites a popular response, which then alters or becomes the next call so that the leading voice always reflects both individual and community. Jody's call will never find a response because of his implicit elitism, which the community recognizes immediately on his arrival in Eatonville:

> JODY: "Ain't got no Mayor! Well, who tells y'all what do do?"
> HICKS: "Nobody. Everybody's grown."

Jody's patriarchal, child-adult or superior-inferior system finds only limited acceptance because it seeks obedience, not contributions.

Janie's storytelling experiences in Belle Glade testify to her potential to issue calls worthy of response and to incorporate those responses in her next call. Eatonville's intuition of her ability results in its invitation to speak during her first evening there (an invitation which Jody quashes); this communal recognition is explicitly established when, in response to her comments on the mule, a bystander comments, " 'Yo' wife is uh born orator, Starks. Us never knowed dat befo'. She put jus' de right words tuh *our* thoughts' " (emphasis added). Janie has talent, experience, flexibility, and communal acceptance. Her participation in storytelling belongs to the Afro-American pattern of call and response; her narration of her own story functions as a call to adventure for other questers. Through Janie, Hurston merges the quest pattern with the Afro-American call and response to form a new experience, a group quest or ascent. *Their Eyes Were Watching God* intimates an Eatonville with Janie and a whole group of Pheobys growing "ten feet tall," traveling in company "tuh de horizon and back," ever constructing and renewing both individual and community.

Ideology and Narrative Form

Houston A. Baker, Jr.

The subtext that emerges from ideological analyses of male and female slave narratives reveals the "traditional" dimensions of such narratives. The commercial, subtextual contours of eighteenth- and nineteenth-century black narratives find their twentieth-century instantiations in works that are frequently called "classic" but that are seldom decoded in the ideological terms of a traditional discourse. It is vital, however—if we are to derive full value from the archaeology of knowledge in discovering a uniquely Afro-American discourse—to recognize the subtextual bonding between a novel such as, say, Zora Neale Hurston's *Their Eyes Were Watching God* and its Afro-American narrative antecedents.

An ideological analysis of *Their Eyes Were Watching God* reveals the endurance and continuity of a discourse that finds its earliest literate manifestations in slave narratives. By revealing the effects of "commercial deportation" and the "economics of slavery" in Hurston's work, ideological analysis makes available, from the standpoint of practical criticism, new meanings. At a more general level of the archaeology of knowledge, the analysis moves us closer to the realization that a Foucaultian "rupture" exists between traditional American history and literary history and an alternative Afro-American discourse. The relationship between Hurston's subtext and that of narratives discussed so far in this chapter provides adequate grounds for postulating a literary history quite different from a

From *Blues, Ideology, and Afro-American Literature: A Vernacular Theory.* © 1984 by the University of Chicago. The University of Chicago Press, 1984.

traditional "American literary history." An examination of *Their Eyes Were Watching God* serves to clarify.

The property designation of an "economics of slavery," as Linda Brent's narrative makes abundantly clear, meant that the owner's sexual gratification (forcefully achieved) was also his profit. The children resulting from such a violation followed the enslaved condition of their mother, becoming property. "Succeeding generations," as we have seen in the previous discussion, translated as "added commodities" for a master's store. The Civil War putatively ended such a commercial lineage.

Zora Neale Hurston's *Their Eyes Were Watching God* traces a fictive history that begins with the concubinage of Nanny to her white owner. The relationship results in the birth of the protagonist's mother. Nanny's experiences have endowed her with what she describes as "a great sermon about colored women sittin' on high." There are, however, no observable phenomena—either in her own progress from day to day or in the surrounding world—to lend credibility to her unarticulated text. She feels that the achievement of a "pulpit" from which to deliver such a sermon is coextensive with the would-be preacher's obtaining actual status on high. In a sense, Nanny conflates the securing of property with effective expression. Having been denied a say in her own fate because she was *property,* she assumes that *only* property enables expression. *Their Eyes Were Watching God* implies that she is unequivocally correct in her judgment and possesses a lucid understanding of the economics of slavery.

The pear tree metaphor—the protagonist's organic fantasy of herself as an orgasmic tree fertilized by careless bees—is a deceptively prominent construct in *Their Eyes Were Watching God*; it leads away from the more significant economic dimensions of the novel so resonantly summed up by Nanny. This romantic construct is, in fact, introduced and maintained in the work by a nostalgic, omnipresent narrator. For Janie's true (authorial?) grounding is in the parodic economics of black, middle-class respectability marked by Logan Killicks and Joe Starks.

These two black men are hardly "careless" bees. Rather, they possess the busyness characteristic of the proverbial bee in another of his manifestations—the "industrious bee." Joe Starks is so intent on imitating the economics of Anglo-American owners that he, paradoxically, manages to obtain a fair abundance of goods; he becomes wealthy, that is to say, by Afro-American standards. It is finally Starks's property, gained through industriousness, that enables Janie's "freedom."

When Starks dies, the protagonist discovers that she is left with both "her widowhood and property." One might suggest that Vergible Woods, or "Tea Cake," the young man who appears to fill the bee's slot in Janie's fantasy, is less a "cause" of freedom than a derivative benefit. Janie confidently asserts of her relationship with Tea Cake: "Dis ain't no business proposition, and no race after property and titles." But she is able to make this claim because she sells Starks's store to finance the relationship. The attentions of a young man, after all, do not in themselves guarantee that a relationship will be a "love game," as the dreadful example of a deceived and stranded Mrs. Annie Tyler proves. It is important to note, however, that the term "Starks's store" disguises, at least in part, the fact that a share of the store as a commodity is surely a function of the protagonist's labor. Janie works for years in the store without receiving more than subsistence provisions. The "surplus value" that accrues from her labor as equity is rightfully hers to dispose of as she chooses.

Their Eyes Were Watching God is, ultimately, a novel that inscribes, in its very form, the mercantile economics that conditioned a "commercial deportation." If Janie is, in the last analysis, a person who delivers a text about "colored women sittin' on high," she is one who delivers this text from a position on high. Her position derives from the petit bourgeois enterprises she has shared with her deceased husband.

To say this is not to minimize the force of Janie's lyrical, autobiographical recall. She can, indeed, be interpreted as a singer who (ontogenetically) recapitulates the blues experience of all black women treated as "mules of the world." She is, indeed, a member of a community of black women. And the expressiveness that she provides in her bleak situation in a racist South is equivalent to the song of Sleepy John Estes which qualifies the bleakness of Winfield Lane.

The descent to the "muck" that provides Janie's artistic apprenticeship among the "common folk" is, nonetheless, unequivocally a function of entrepreneurial, capitalistic economic exchange. (Zora Hurston's own trip to the South to collect her people's lore was financed by a rich white patron, Mrs. Rufus Osgood Mason.) The duality suggested by Janie's blues song and its capitalistic enabling conditions is simply one manifestation, finally, of the general dilemma of the Afro-American artist born from an economics of slavery.

The protagonist of *Their Eyes Were Watching God* is known to her childhood cohorts as "Alphabet" because she has been given so many "different names." Likewise, the Afro-American artist has been marginally situated in American culture, without a single, definite name, but embodying within herself the possibility of all names—the alphabet. The only way to shape a *profitable*, expressive identity in such a situation is to play on possibilities—to divide one's self, as Janie does, into "public" and "private" personalities.

In the example of the Afro-American artist, this has meant shaping an expression to fit the marketplace—an act kin to Janie's voluntary silences and seeming complicity in the public, commercial world of her husband's store. Once adequate finances are secured, however, the alphabet can be transformed (as Vassa, Douglass, and Jacobs all demonstrate) into the manifold combinations that make for expressive authenticity. Janie, for example, goes South, gains experience, and returns to the communal landscape of Eatonville as a storyteller and blues singer par excellence.

Her striking expressiveness within the confines of Eatonville, however, is framed, or bracketed, by the bourgeois economics of Anglo-America. The terrible close of her arcadian sojourn on the "muck" is a return, in the company of a rabidly infected Tea Cake, to a viciously segregated world. A sign of the type of relationships sanctioned by such a world is the mad (male) dog atop the back of a terrified female cow. (The patriarchal economics of Brent's work come forcefully to mind.) Given a world implied by such a sign, and by the Jim Crow ethics of the urban environs that Janie and Tea Cake enter, where can the protagonist sing her newly found song of the folk? Having discovered the terrible boundaries on her freedom and its expressive potentialities, she returns to sing to an exclusively black audience.

An ideological reading of *Their Eyes Were Watching God,* thus, claims that the novel inscribes not only the economics signaled by commercial deportation but also the economic contours of the Afro-American artist's dilemma. Nanny, Janie's grandmother, is resoundingly correct in her conclusion that the pulpit (a propertied position on high ground) is a prerequisite for a stirring sermon. From an ideological perspective, Hurston's novel is a commentary on the continuing necessity for Afro-Americans to observe property relationships and to negotiate the restrictions sanctioned by the economics of slavery if they would achieve expressive wholeness.

Janie does not *transcend* the conditions occasioned by commercial deportation; she, like the narrative protagonists of her discursive predecessors, adapts profitably to them. And like many thousands gone before, she sings resonantly about the bleak fate and narrow straits that such an adaptation mandates. Her song is not identical to the unmediated, folk expression of those many thousands gone before. Despite its authentic dialectal transcription, her blues for the townfolk's consumption are made possible—financed, as it were—by a bourgeois economics. They are, in this respect, allied to entertainment. The full contours of the expressive dilemma she so successfully negotiates become even clearer in the analysis of such succeeding examples of Afro-American narrative as Ralph Ellison's *Invisible Man*—a work to which I will turn [elsewhere].

If my judgment of Hurston's work fails to accord with more romantic readings of *Their Eyes Were Watching God,* at least it possesses the virtue of introducing essential, traditional, subtextual dimensions of Afro-American discourse into the universe surrounding the novel. It is difficult to see how economic and expressive-artistic considerations can be ignored in treating a narrative that signals its own origination in a commercial deportation. Surely *economics,* conceived in terms of an ideology of narrative form like that represented in the foregoing analyses, has much to contribute to an understanding of the classic works of an expressive tradition grounded in the economics of slavery.

The value of the archaeology of knowledge and the ideological perspective it occasions does not lie exclusively in an expanded, practical criticism of Afro-American narratives, however. The specific governing statements I have introduced in this chapter could be replaced (and an entirely different discursive structure constituted) by alternative governing statements. "Territorial invasion," for instance, might serve especially well to structure a Chicano or Native American literary history. The archaeology of knowledge vis-à-vis American literary history need not be confined to a single expressive frame of reference.

The greater utility of archaeology consists in the fact that it asks questions about *the nature and method of history and literary history in themselves,* bringing into question the role of ideology in literary history and literary study in general. The mode of thought occasioned by Foucault's project, therefore, might well be employed to substitute other American constructs for "Afro-American history" and "Afro-American literary history." But such displacements could not occur without further raising the kinds of questions and motivating the type of analyses that have characterized the foregoing discussion.

Metaphor, Metonymy and Voice in *Their Eyes Were Watching God*

Barbara Johnson

Not so very long ago, metaphor and metonymy burst into prominence as the salt and pepper, the Laurel and Hardy, the Yin and Yang, and often the Scylla and Charybdis of literary theory. Then, just as quickly, this cosmic couple passed out of fashion again. How did it happen that such an arcane rhetorical opposition was able to acquire the brief but powerful privilege of dividing and naming the whole of human reality, from Mommy and Daddy or Symptom and Desire all the way to God and Country or Beautiful Lie and Sober Lucidity?

The contemporary sense of the opposition between metaphor and metonymy was first formulated by Roman Jakobson in an article entitled "Two Aspects of Language and Two Types of Aphasic Disturbances." That article, first published in English in 1956, derives much of its celebrity from the central place accorded by the French structuralists to the 1963 translation of a selection of Jakobson's work, entitled *Essais linguistiques,* which included the aphasia study. The words "metaphor" and "metonymy" are not, of course, of twentieth-century coinage: they are classical tropes traditionally defined as the substitution of a figurative expression for a literal or proper one. In metaphor, the substitution is based on resemblance or analogy; in metonymy, it is based on a relation or association other than that of similarity (cause and effect, container and contained, proper name and qualities or works associated with it, place and event or institution, instrument and user, etc.). The use of the name "Camelot" to refer to John Kennedy's

From *Black Literature and Literary Theory,* edited by Henry Louis Gates, Jr. © 1984 by Methuen & Co., Inc.

Washington is thus an example of metaphor, since it implies an analogy between Kennedy's world and King Arthur's, while the use of the word "Watergate" to refer to the scandal that ended Richard Nixon's presidency is a metonymy, since it transfers the name of an arbitrary place of origin onto a whole sequence of subsequent events.

Jakobson's use of the two terms is an extension and polarization of their classical definitions. In studying patterns of aphasia (speech dysfunction), Jakobson found that they fell into two main categories: similarity disorders and contiguity disorders. In the former, grammatical contexture and lateral associations remain while synonymity drops out; in the latter, heaps of word substitutes are kept while grammar and connectedness vanish. Jakobson concludes:

> The development of a discourse may take place along two different semantic lines: one topic may lead to another either through their similarity or through their contiguity. The metaphoric way would be the most appropriate term for the first case and the metonymic way for the second, since they find their most condensed expression in metaphor and metonymy respectively. In aphasia one or the other of these two processes is restricted or totally blocked—an effect which makes the study of aphasia particularly illuminating for the linguist. In normal verbal behavior both processes are continually operative, but careful observation will reveal that under the influence of a cultural pattern, personality, and verbal style, preference is given to one of the two processes over the other.
>
> In a well-known psychological test, children are confronted with some noun and told to utter the first verbal response that comes into their heads. In this experiment two opposite linguistic predilections are invariably exhibited: the response is intended either as a substitute for, or as a complement to the stimulus. In the latter case the stimulus and the response together form a proper syntactic construction, most usually a sentence. These two types of reaction have been labeled substitutive and predicative.
>
> To the stimulus *hut* one response was *burnt out*; another, *is a poor little house*. Both reactions are predicative; but the first creates a purely narrative context, while in the second there is a double connection with the subject *hut:* on the one hand, a positional (namely, syntactic) contiguity, and on the other a semantic similarity.

The same stimulus produced the following substitutive reactions: the tautology *hut;* the synonyms *cabin* and *hovel;* the antonym *palace,* and the metaphors *den* and *burrow.* The capacity of two words to replace one another is an instance of positional similarity, and, in addition, all these responses are linked to the stimulus by semantic similarity (or contrast). Metonymical responses to the same stimulus, such as *thatch, litter,* or *poverty,* combine and contrast the positional similarity with semantic contiguity.

In manipulating these two kinds of connection (similarity and contiguity) in both their aspects (positional and semantic)—selecting, combining, and ranking them—an individual exhibits his personal style, his verbal predilections and preferences.

Two problems immediately arise that render the opposition between metaphor and metonymy at once more interesting and more problematic than at first appears. The first is that there are not two poles here but four: similarity, contiguity, semantic connection, and syntactic connection. A more adequate representation of these oppositions can be schematized as in Figure 1. Jakobson's contention that poetry is a syntactic extension of metaphor ("The poetic function projects the principle of equivalence from the axis of selection into the axis of combination"), while realist narrative is an extension of metonymy, can be added to the graph as in Figure 2.

The second problem that arises in any attempt to apply the metaphor/metonymy distinction is that it is often very hard to tell the two apart. In Ronsard's poem "Mignonne, allons voir si la rose . . .," the speaker invites the lady to go for a walk with him (the walk being an example of contiguity) to see a rose which, once beautiful (like the lady), is now withered (as the lady will eventually be): the day must therefore be seized. The metonymic proximity to the flower is designed solely to reveal the metaphoric point of the poem: enjoy life while you still bloom. The tendency of contiguity to become overlaid by similarity and vice versa may be summed up in the

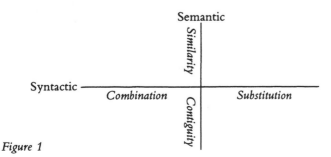

Figure 1

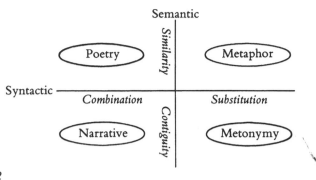

Figure 2

proverb, "Birds of a feather flock together"—"Qui se ressemble s'assemble." One has only to think of the applicability of this proverb to the composition of neighborhoods in America'to realize that the question of the separability of similarity from contiguity may have considerable political implications. The controversy surrounding the expression "legionnaires' disease" provides a more comical example: while the name of the disease derives solely from the contingent fact that its first victims were at an American Legion Convention, and is thus a metonymy, the fear that it will take on a metaphoric color—that a belief in some natural connection or similarity may thereby be propagated between legionnaires and the disease—has led spokesmen for the legionnaires to attempt to have the malady renamed. And finally, in the sentence "The White House denied the charges," one might ask whether the place name is a purely contiguous metonymy for the presidency, or whether the whiteness of the house isn't somehow metaphorically connected to the whiteness of its inhabitant.

One final prefatory remark about the metaphor/metonymy distinction: far from being a neutral opposition between equals, these two tropes have always stood in hierarchical relation to each other. From Aristotle to George Lakoff, metaphor has always, in the Western tradition, had the privilege of revealing unexpected truth. As Aristotle puts it: "Midway between the unintelligible and the commonplace, it is a metaphor which most produces knowledge." Paul de Man summarizes the preference for metaphor over metonymy by aligning analogy with necessity and contiguity with chance: "The inference of identity and totality that is constitutive of metaphor is lacking in the purely relational metonymic contact: an element of truth is involved in taking Achilles for a lion but none in taking Mr Ford for a motor car." De Man then goes on to reveal this "element of truth" as the product of a purely rhetorical—and ultimately metonymical—sleight of hand, thus overturning the traditional hierarchy and deconstructing the very basis for the seductiveness and privilege of metaphor.

I should like now to turn to the work of an author acutely conscious of, and superbly skilled in, the seductiveness and complexity of metaphor as privileged trope and trope of privilege. Zora Neale Hurston, novelist, folklorist, essayist, anthropologist, and Harlem Renaissance personality, cut her teeth on figurative language during the tale-telling or "lying" sessions that took place on a store porch in the all-black town of Eatonville, Florida, where she was born around 1901. She devoted her life to the task of recording, preserving, novelizing, and analyzing the patterns of speech and thought of the rural black South and related cultures. At the same time, she deplored the appropriation, dilution, and commodification of black culture (through spirituals, jazz, etc.) by the pre-Depression white world, and she constantly tried to explain the difference between a reified "art" and a living culture in which the distinctions between spectator and spectacle, rehearsal and performance, experience and representation, are not fixed. "Folklore," she wrote, "is the arts of the people before they find out that there is such a thing as art."

> Folklore does not belong to any special area, time, nor people. It is a world and an ageless thing, so let us look at it from that viewpoint. It is the boiled down juice of human living and when one phase of it passes another begins which shall in turn give way before a successor.
>
> Culture is a forced march on the near and the obvious. . . . The intelligent mind uses up a great part of its lifespan trying to awaken its consciousness sufficiently to comprehend that which is plainly there before it. Every generation or so some individual with extra keen perception grasps something of the obvious about us and hitches the human race forward slightly by a new "law." Millions of things had been falling on men for thousands of years before the falling apple hit Newton on the head and he saw the law of gravity.

Through this strategic description of the folkloric heart of scientific law, Hurston dramatizes the predicament not only of the anthropologist but also of the novelist: both are caught between the (metaphorical) urge to universalize or totalize and the knowledge that it is precisely "the near and the obvious" that will never be grasped once and for all but will only be (metonymically) named and renamed, as different things successively strike different heads. I shall return to this problem of universality at the end of this essay, but first I should like to take a close look at some of the figurative operations at work in Hurston's best-known novel, *Their Eyes Were Watching God.*

The novel presents, in a combination of first- and third-person narration, the story of Janie Crawford and her three successive husbands. The first, Logan Killicks, is chosen by Janie's grandmother for his sixty acres and as a socially secure harbor for Janie's awakening sexuality. When Janie realizes that love does not automatically follow upon marriage and that Killicks completely lacks imagination, she decides to run off with ambitious, smart-talking, stylishly dressed Joe Starks, who is headed for a new all-black town where he hopes to become what he calls a "big voice." Later, as mayor and store owner of the town, he proudly raises Janie to a pedestal of property and propriety. Because this involves her submission to his idea of what a mayor's wife should be, Janie soon finds her pedestal to be a straitjacket, particularly when it involves her exclusion—both as speaker and as listener—from the tale-telling sessions on the store porch and at the mock funeral of a mule. Little by little, Janie begins to talk back to Joe, finally insulting him so profoundly that, in a sense, he dies of it. Some time later, into Janie's life walks Tea Cake Woods, whose first act is to teach Janie how to play checkers. "Somebody wanted her to play," says the text in free indirect discourse; "Somebody thought it natural for her to play." Thus begins a joyous liberation from the rigidities of status, image, and property—one of the most beautiful and convincing love stories in any literature. In a series of courtship dances, appearances, and disappearances, Tea Cake succeeds in fulfilling Janie's dream of "a bee for her blossom." Tea Cake, unlike Joe and Logan, regards money and work as worth only the amount of play and enjoyment they make possible. He gains and loses money unpredictably until he and Janie begin working side by side picking beans on "the muck" in the Florida Everglades. This idyll of pleasure, work, and equality ends dramatically with a hurricane during which Tea Cake, while saving Janie's life, is bitten by a rabid dog. When Tea Cake's subsequent hydrophobia transforms him into a wild and violent animal, Janie is forced to shoot him in self-defense. Acquitted of murder by an all-white jury, Janie returns to Eatonville, where she tells her story to her friend Phoeby Watson.

The passage on which I should like to concentrate both describes and dramatizes, in its figurative structure, a crucial turning point in Janie's relation to Joe and to herself. The passage follows an argument over what Janie has done with a bill of lading, during which Janie shouts, "You sho loves to tell me whut to do, but Ah can't tell you nothin' Ah see!"

"Dat's 'cause you need tellin'," he rejoined hotly. "It would be pitiful if Ah didn't. Somebody got to think for women and chillun and chickens and cows. I god, they sho don't think none theirselves."

"Ah knows uh few things, and womenfolks thinks sometimes too!"

"Aw naw they don't. They just think they's thinkin'. When Ah see one thing Ah understands ten. You see ten things and don't understand one."

Times and scenes like that put Janie to thinking about the inside state of her marriage. Time came when she fought back with her tongue as best she could, but it didn't do her any good. It just made Joe do more. He wanted her submission and he'd keep on fighting until he felt he had it.

So gradually, she pressed her teeth together and learned how to hush. The spirit of the marriage left the bedroom and took to living in the parlor. It was there to shake hands whenever company came to visit, but it never went back inside the bedroom again. So she put something in there to represent the spirit like a Virgin Mary image in a church. The bed was no longer a daisy-field for her and Joe to play in. It was a place where she went and laid down when she was sleepy and tired.

She wasn't petal-open anymore with him. She was twenty-four and seven years married when she knew. She found that out one day when he slapped her face in the kitchen. It happened over one of those dinners that chasten all women sometimes. They plan and they fix and they do, and then some kitchen-dwelling fiend slips a scrochy, soggy, tasteless mess into their pots and pans. Janie was a good cook, and Joe had looked forward to his dinner as a refuge from other things. So when the bread didn't rise and the fish wasn't quite done at the bone, and the rice was scorched, he slapped Janie until she had a ringing sound in her ears and told her about her brains before he stalked on back to the store.

Janie stood where he left her for unmeasured time and thought. She stood there until something fell off the shelf inside her. Then she went inside there to see what it was. It was her image of Jody tumbled down and shattered. But looking at it she saw that it never was the flesh and blood figure of her dreams. Just something she had grabbed up to drape her dreams over. In a way she turned her back upon the image where it lay and looked further. She had no more blossomy openings dusting pollen over her man, neither any glistening young fruit where the petals used to be. She found that she had a host of thoughts she had never expressed to him, and numerous emotions she had never let Jody know about. Things packed up and put away in parts of her heart where he could never find them. She was saving up feelings for some man she had never seen. She had an inside and an outside now and suddenly she knew how not to mix them.

This opposition between an inside and an outside is a standard way of describing the nature of a rhetorical figure. The vehicle, or surface meaning, is seen as enclosing an inner tenor, or figurative meaning. This relation can be pictured somewhat facetiously as a gilded carriage—the vehicle—containing Luciano Pavarotti, the tenor. Within the passage cited from *Their Eyes Were Watching God,* I should like to concentrate on the two paragraphs that begin respectively "So gradually" and "Janie stood where he left her." In these two paragraphs Hurston plays a number of interesting variations on the inside/outside opposition.

In both paragraphs, a relation is set up between an inner "image" and outward, domestic space. The parlor, bedroom, and store full of shelves already exist in the narrative space of the novel: they are figures drawn metonymically from the familiar contiguous surroundings. Each of these paragraphs recounts a little narrative of, and within, its own figurative terms. In the first, the inner spirit of the marriage moves outward from the bedroom to the parlor, cutting itself off from its proper place, and replacing itself with an image of virginity, the antithesis of marriage. Although Joe is constantly exclaiming, "I god, Janie," he will not be as successful as his namesake in uniting with the Virgin Mary. Indeed, it is his godlike self-image that forces Janie to retreat to virginity. The entire paragraph is an externalization of Janie's feelings onto the outer surroundings in the form of a narrative of movement from private to public space. While the whole of the figure relates metaphorically, analogically, to the marital situation it is designed to express, it reveals the marriage space to be metonymical, a movement through a series of contiguous rooms. It is a narrative not of union but of separation centered on an image not of conjugality but of virginity.

In the second passage, just after the slap, Janie is standing, thinking, until something "fell off the shelf inside her." Janie's "inside" is here represented as a store that she then goes in to inspect. While the former paragraph was an externalization of the inner, here we find an internalization of the outer: Janie's inner self resembles a store. The material for this metaphor is drawn from the narrative world of contiguity: the store is the place where Joe has set himself up as lord, master, and proprietor. But here Jody's image is broken, and reveals itself never to have been a metaphor but only a metonymy of Janie's dream: "looking at it she saw that it never was the flesh and blood figure of her dreams. Just something she had grabbed up to drape her dreams over."

What we find in juxtaposing these two figural mininarratives is a kind of chiasmus, or crossover, in which the first paragraph presents an externalization of the inner, a metaphorically grounded metonymy, while the second paragraph presents an internalization of the outer, or a metonymically grounded metaphor. In both cases, the quotient of the operation is the revelation of a false or discordant "image." Janie's image, as Virgin Mary, acquires a new intactness, while Joe's lies shattered on the floor. The reversals operated by the chiasmus map out a reversal of the power relations between Janie and Joe. Henceforth, Janie will grow in power and resistance, while Joe deteriorates both in his body and in his public image.

The moral of these two figural tales is rich with implications: "She had an inside and an outside now and suddenly she knew how not to mix them." On the one hand, this means that she knew how to keep the inside and the outside separate without trying to blend or merge them into one unified identity. On the other hand it means that she has stepped irrevocably into the necessity of figurative language, where inside and outside are never the same. It is from this point on in the novel that Janie, paradoxically, begins to speak. And it is by means of a devastating figure—"You look like the change of life"—that she wounds Jody to the quick. Janie's acquisition of the power of voice thus grows not out of her identity but out of her division into inside and outside. Knowing how not to mix them is knowing that articulate language requires the co-presence of two distinct poles, not their collapse into oneness.

This, of course, is what Jakobson concludes in his discussion of metaphor and metonymy. For it must be remembered that what is at stake in the maintenance of both sides—metaphor and metonymy, inside and outside—is the very possibility of speaking at all. The reduction of a discourse to oneness, identity—in Janie's case, the reduction of woman to mayor's wife—has as its necessary consequence aphasia, silence, the loss of the ability to speak: "she pressed her teeth together and learned how to hush."

What has gone unnoticed in theoretical discussions of Jakobson's article is that behind the metaphor/metonymy distinction lies the much more serious distinction between speech and aphasia, between silence and the capacity to articulate one's own voice. To privilege *either* metaphor *or* metonymy is thus to run the risk of producing an increasingly aphasic *critical* discourse. If both, or all four, poles must be operative in order for speech to function fully, then the very notion of an "authentic voice" must be redefined. Far from being an expression of Janie's new wholeness or identity as a character, Janie's increasing ability to speak grows out of her ability not to mix inside with outside, not to pretend that there is no difference, but to assume and articulate the incompatible forces involved in her own division. The sign of an authentic voice is thus not self-identity but self-difference.

The search for wholeness, oneness, universality, and totalization can nevertheless never be put to rest. However rich, healthy, or lucid fragmentation and division may be, narrative seems to have trouble resting content with it, as though a story could not recognize its own end as anything other than a moment of totalization—even when what is totalized is loss. The ending of *Their Eyes Were Watching God* is no exception:

> Of course [Tea Cake] wasn't dead. He could never be dead until she herself had finished feeling and thinking. The kiss of his memory made pictures of love and light against the wall. Here was peace. She pulled in her horizon like a great fish-net. Pulled it from around the waist of the world and draped it over her shoulder. So much of life in its meshes! She called in her soul to come and see.

The horizon, with all of life caught in its meshes, is here pulled into the self as a gesture of total recuperation and peace. It is as though self-division could be healed over at last, but only at the cost of a radical loss of the other.

This hope for some ultimate unity and peace seems to structure the very sense of an ending as such, whether that of a novel or that of a work of literary criticism. At the opposite end of the "canonical" scale, one finds it, for example, in the last chapter of Erich Auerbach's *Mimesis*, perhaps the greatest of modern monuments to the European literary canon. That final chapter, entitled "The Brown Stocking" after the stocking that Virginia Woolf's Mrs Ramsay is knitting in *To the Lighthouse*, is a description of certain narrative tendencies in the modern novel: "multipersonal representation of consciousness, time strata, disintegration of the continuity of exterior events, shifting of narrative viewpoint," etc.

Let us begin with a tendency which is particularly striking in our text from Virginia Woolf. She holds to minor, unimpressive, random events: measuring the stocking, a fragment of a conversation with the maid, a telephone call. Great changes, exterior turning points, let alone catastrophes, do not occur.

Auerbach concludes his discussion of the modernists' preoccupation with the minor, the trivial, and the marginal by saying:

> It is precisely the random moment which is comparatively independent of the controversial and unstable orders over which men fight and despair. . . . The more numerous, varied, and simple the people are who appear as subjects of such random moments, the more effectively must what they have in common shine forth. . . . So the complicated process of dissolution which led to fragmentation of the exterior action, to reflection of consciousness, and to stratification of time seems to be tending toward a very simple solution. Perhaps it will be too simple to please those who, despite all its dangers and catastrophes, admire and love our epoch for the sake of its abundance of life and the incomparable historical vantage point which it affords. But they are few in number, and probably they will not live to see much more than the first forewarnings of the approaching unification and simplication.

Never has the desire to transform fragmentation into unity been expressed so succinctly and authoritatively—indeed, almost prophetically. One cannot help but wonder, though, whether the force of this desire has not been provoked by the fact that the primary text it wishes to unify and simplify was written by a woman. What Auerbach calls "minor, unimpressive, random events"—measuring a stocking, conversing with the maid, answering the phone—can all be identified as conventional *women*'s activities. "Great changes," "exterior turning points," and "catastrophes" have been the stuff of heroic *male* literature. Even plot itself—up until *Madame Bovary*, at least—has been conceived as the doings of those who do *not* stay at home, i.e., men. Auerbach's urge to unify and simplify is an urge to resubsume female difference under the category of the universal, which has always been unavowedly male. The random, the trivial, and the marginal will simply be added to the list of things all *men* have in common.

If "unification and simplification" is the privilege and province of the male, it is also, in America, the privilege and province of the white. If the woman's voice, to be authentic, must incorporate and articulate division and self-difference, so, too, has Afro-American literature always had to assume its double-voicedness. As Henry Louis Gates, Jr., puts it in "Criticism in the Jungle":

> In the instance of the writer of African descent, her or his texts occupy spaces in at least two traditions—the individual's European or American literary tradition, and one of the three related but distinct black traditions. The "heritage" of each black text written in a Western language, then, is a double heritage, two-toned, as it were. . . . Each utterance, then, is double-voiced.

This is a reformulation of W. E. B. DuBois's famous image of the "veil" that divides the black American in two:

> The Negro is a sort of seventh son, born with a veil, and gifted with second sight in this American world,—a world which yields him no true self-consciousness, but only lets him see himself through the revelation of the other world. It is a peculiar sensation, this double-consciousness, this sense of always looking at one's self through the eyes of others, of measuring one's soul by the tape of a world that looks on in amused contempt and pity. One ever feels his twoness—an American, a Negro; two souls, two thoughts, two unreconciled strivings; two warring ideals in one dark body, whose dogged strength alone keeps it from being torn asunder.
>
> The history of the American Negro is the history of this strife,—this longing to attain self-conscious manhood, to merge his double self into a better and truer self.

James Weldon Johnson, in his *Autobiography of an Ex-Colored Man*, puts it this way:

> This is the dwarfing, warping, distorting influence which operates upon each and every colored man in the United States. He is forced to take his outlook on all things, not from the viewpoint of a citizen, or a man, or even a human being, but from the view-point of a *colored* man. . . . This gives to every colored man, in proportion to his intellectuality, a sort of dual personality.

What is striking about the above two quotations is that they both assume without question that the black subject is male. The black woman is totally invisible in these descriptions of the black dilemma. Richard Wright, in his review of *Their Eyes Were Watching God,* makes it plain that for him, too, the black female experience is nonexistent. The novel, says Wright, lacks

> a basic idea or theme that lends itself to significant interpretation.
> . . . [Hurston's] dialogue manages to catch the psychological movements of the Negro folk-mind in their pure simplicity, but that's as far as it goes. . . . The sensory sweep of her novel carries no theme, no message, no thought.

No message, no theme, no thought: the full range of questions and experiences of Janie's life are as invisible to a mind steeped in maleness as Ellison's Invisible Man is to minds steeped in whiteness. If the black *man*'s soul is divided in two, what can be said of the black woman's? Here again, what is constantly seen exclusively in terms of a binary opposition—black versus white, man versus woman—must be redrawn at least as a tetrapolar structure (see Figure 3). What happens in the case of a black woman is that the four quadrants are constantly being collapsed into two. Hurston's work is often called nonpolitical simply because readers of Afro-American literature tend to look for confrontational *racial* politics, not sexual politics. If the black woman voices opposition to male domination, she is often seen as a traitor to the cause of racial justice. But, if she sides with black men against white oppression, she often winds up having to accept her position within the Black Power movement as, in Stokely Carmichael's words, "prone." This impossible position between two oppositions is what I think Hurston intends when, at the end of the novel, she represents Janie as acquitted of the murder of Tea Cake by an all-white jury but condemned by her fellow blacks. This is not out of a "lack of bitterness toward whites," as one reader would have it, but rather out of a knowledge of the standards of male dominance that pervade both the black and the white worlds. The black crowd at the trial murmurs, "Tea Cake was a good boy. He had been

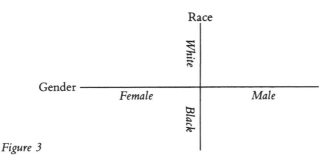

Figure 3

good to that woman. No nigger woman ain't never been treated no better."
As Janie's grandmother puts it early in the novel:

> "Honey, de white man is de ruler of everything as fur as Ah
> been able tuh find out. Maybe it's some place way off in de
> ocean where de black man is in power, but we don't know
> nothin' but what we see. So de white man throw down de load
> and tell de nigger man tuh pick it up. He pick it up because he
> have to, but he don't tote it. He hand it to his womenfolks. De
> nigger woman is de mule uh de world so fur as Ah can see."

In a very persuasive book on black women and feminism entitled *Ain't
I a Woman,* Bell Hooks (Gloria Watkins) discusses the ways in which black
women suffer from both sexism and racism within the very movements
whose ostensible purpose is to set them free. Watkins argues that "black
woman" has never been considered a separate, distinct category with a
history and complexity of its own. When a president appoints a black
woman to a cabinet post, for example, he does not feel he is appointing a
person belonging to the category "black woman"; he is appointing a person
who belongs *both* to the category "black" *and* to the category "woman,"
and is thus killing two birds with one stone. Watkins says of the analogy
often drawn—particularly by white feminists—between blacks and women:

> Since analogies derive their power, their appeal, and their very
> reason for being from the sense of two disparate phenomena
> having been brought closer together, for white women to ac-
> knowledge the overlap between the terms "blacks" and
> "women" (that is, the existence of black women) would render
> this analogy unnecessary. By continuously making this analogy,
> they unwittingly suggest that to them the term "women" is
> synonymous with "white women" and the term "blacks" syn-
> onymous with "black men."

The very existence of black women thus disappears from an analogical
discourse designed to express the types of oppression from which black
women have the most to suffer.

In the current hierarchical view of things, this tetrapolar graph can be
filled in as in Figure 4. The black woman is both invisible and ubiquitous:
never seen in her own right but forever appropriated by the others for their
own ends.

Ultimately, though, this mapping of tetrapolar differences is itself a
fantasy of universality. Are all the members of each quadrant the same?

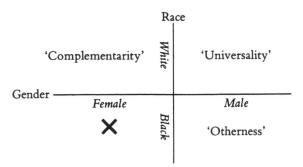

Figure 4

Where are the nations, the regions, the religions, the classes, the professions? Where are the other races, the interracial subdivisions? How can the human world be totalized, even as a field of divisions? In the following quotation from Zora Neale Hurston's autobiography, we see that even the *same* black woman can express self-division in two completely different ways:

Work was to be all of me, so I said. . . . I had finished that phase of research and was considering writing my first book, when I met the man who was really to lay me by the heels. . . .

He was tall, dark brown, magnificently built, with a beautifully modeled back head. His profile was strong and good. The nose and lips were especially good front and side. But his looks only drew my eyes in the beginning. I did not fall in love with him just for that. He had a fine mind and that intrigued me. When a man keeps beating me to the draw mentally, he begins to get glamorous. . . . His intellect got me first for I am the kind of woman that likes to move on mentally from point to point, and I like for my man to be there way ahead of me. . . .

His great desire was to do for me. *Please* let him be a *man!* . . .

That very manliness, sweet as it was, made us both suffer. My career balked the completeness of his ideal. I really wanted to conform, but it was impossible. To me there was no conflict. My work was one thing, and he was all the rest. But I could not make him see that. Nothing must be in my life but himself. . . . We could not leave each other alone, and we could not shield each other from hurt. . . . In the midst of this, I received my Guggenheim Fellowship. This was my chance to release him, and fight myself free from my obsession. He would get over me in a few months and go on to be a very big man. So I sailed off to Jamaica [and] pitched in to work hard on my research to smother my feelings. But the thing would not down. The plot was far from the circumstances, but I tried to embalm all the tenderness of my passion for him in *Their Eyes Were Watching God*.

The plot is indeed far from the circumstances, and, what is even more striking, it is lived by what seems to be a completely different woman. While Janie struggles to attain equal respect *within* a relation to a man, Zora readily submits to the pleasures of submission yet struggles to establish the legitimacy of a professional life *outside* the love relation. The female voice may be universally described as divided, but it must be recognized as divided in a multitude of ways.

There is no point of view from which the universal characteristics of the human, or of the woman, or of the black woman, or even of Zora Neale Hurston, can be selected and totalized. Unification and simplification are fantasies of domination, not understanding.

The task of the writer, then, would seem to be to narrate both the appeal and the injustice of universalization, in a voice that assumes and articulates its own, ever differing self-difference. In the opening pages of *Their Eyes Were Watching God* we find, indeed, a brilliant and subtle transition from the seduction of a universal language through a progressive de-universalization that ends in the exclusion of the very protagonist herself. The book begins:

> Ships at a distance have every man's wish on board. For some they come in with the tide. For others they sail forever on the horizon, never out of sight, never landing until the Watcher turns his eyes away in resignation, his dreams mocked to death by Time. That is the life of men.
>
> Now, women forget all those things they don't want to remember, and remember everything they don't want to forget. The dream is the truth. Then they act and do things accordingly.
>
> So the beginning of this was a woman, and she had come back from burying the dead. Not the dead of sick and ailing with friends at the pillow and the feet. She had come back from the sodden and the bloated; the sudden dead, their eyes flung wide open in judgment.
>
> The people all saw her come because it was sundown.

At this point Janie crosses center stage and goes out, while the people, the "bander log," pass judgment on her. The viewpoint has moved from "every man" to "men" to "women" to "a woman" to an absence commented on by "words without masters," the gossip of the front porch. When Janie begins to speak, even the universalizing category of "standard English" gives way to the careful representation of dialect. The narrative voice in this novel expresses its own self-division by shifts between first and third person, standard English, and dialect. This self-division culminates in the frequent use of free indirect discourse, in which, as Henry Louis Gates, Jr., points out, the inside/outside boundaries between narrator and character, between standard and individual, are both transgressed and preserved, making it impossible to identify and totalize either the subject or the nature of discourse.

Narrative, it seems, is an endless fishing expedition with the horizon as both the net and the fish, the big one that always gets away. The meshes continually enclose and let escape, tear open, and mend up again. Mrs Ramsay never finishes the brown stocking. A woman's work is never done. Penelope's weaving is nightly re-unraveled. The porch never stops passing the world through its mouth. The process of de-universalization can never, universally, be completed.

Orality and Textuality in *Their Eyes Were Watching God*

Elizabeth Meese

Hurston, as a black woman, poses a double threat. In her article, " 'This Infinity of Conscious Pain': Zora Neale Hurston and the Black Female Literary Tradition," Lorraine Bethel assesses Hurston's place within literature in terms of a confluence of oppressive forces: "The codification of Blackness and femaleness by whites and males is contained in the terms 'thinking like a woman' and 'acting like a nigger,' both based on the premise that there are typically negative Black and female ways of acting and thinking. Therefore, the most pejorative concept in the white male world view would be thinking and acting like a 'nigger woman.' This is useful for understanding literary criticism of Hurston's works, which often attacks her personally for simply conducting herself as what she was: a Black woman." By insisting on her right to be a "Black woman," free from prescribed roles, Hurston was perhaps as immediately intimidating to black men as to white. Because she was a black woman without independent resources, her white patrons undoubtedly experienced a more secure relationship based on dominance. Hurston necessarily tolerated the situation, although it did little to earn public praise for her literary accomplishments when she struggled to tell her own story rather than the one whites constructed for her to tell. Within this arena of sexual and racial conflict, Hurston's literary reputation suffered.

Over the years, critics have commented variously on the central theme of *Their Eyes Were Watching God*. Washington argues that the novel's most

---

From *Crossing the Double Cross: The Practice of Feminist Criticism* © 1986 by the University of North Carolina Press.

powerful theme "is Janie's search for identity, an identity which finally begins to take shape as she throws off the false images which have been thrust upon her becasuse she is both black and woman in a society where neither is allowed to exist naturally and freely." Hurston expresses this theme, Washington maintains, through the images of the horizon and the pear tree, the former symbolizing Janie's personal, individual quest, the latter, her search for fulfillment through union with another. Ann Rayson argues similarly that Hurston chooses "becoming" rather than "being" as the principal focus of her fiction, suggesting a parallel with Ellison's protagonist, who says, "the end is the beginning." While Rayson's comment reveals her sensitivity to Hurston's choice of narrative strategy, she does not examine that sense of circularity or the reasons underlying Hurston's choice. The question of creating form through narrative technique, which serves as the basis for Janie's deconstruction of the effects of power, provides the focus for my discussion of *Their Eyes Were Watching God* and offers one way of relating this work to those of other feminist writers.

The puzzle of the novel's structure is inseparable from considerations of its theme. Despite Larry Neal's contention that "Zora Neale Hurston was not an especially philosophical person," Hurston employs a narrative strategy that is culturally, philosophically, and aesthetically complex. This complexity reveals itself through Hurston's decision to retell the story rather than to tell it. Barbara Christian makes an important observation about this choice, which the scope of her book does not permit her to develop: "*Their Eyes Were Watching God* is a story within a story. Janie Stark tells the story of her childhood, her life, and her loves to her best friend, Phoebe [*sic*], and to the community to which she has just returned. This aspect of the novel is critical to its substance, for Janie Stark is not an individual in a vacuum; she is an intrinsic part of a community, and she brings her life and its richness, joys, and sorrows back to it. As it has helped to form her, so she also helps to form it." Lillie Howard, however, finds fault with Hurston's method and maintains that "the story is rather awkwardly told by both the heroine, Janie Crawford, and an omniscient narrator, and is revealed, for the most part, in a flashback to Janie's best friend, Phoeby Watson. The narrative is awkward in some places because much of what Janie tells Phoeby, Phoeby must already know, partly because she is Janie's best friend, and partly because Phoeby was a part of Eatonville just as Janie was." It is neither through accident nor uncalculated device that Janie's story is retold rather than told. Why does Hurston choose to do this when, as Howard correctly observes, Phoeby—the audience for the fiction within the fiction—surely knows much of the story she is being told? The value of the approach as strategy exists in what Hurston accomplishes through its use; here as well rests much of the novel's significance for feminist readers today.

Hurston's artistic method displays a keen awareness of the performative quality of fiction as it emerges from the tradition of oral narrative, as well as a clever consciousness of the storyteller-writer's role in constructing the history of a people through language. Her brilliant use of dialect, specifying pride and ownership, lends credibility to the novel's claim as a work for the black community. It is a testament to the power and beauty of blackness. Hurston is culturally and artistically at ease with the narrative convention of retelling the tale, just as her character Janie has grown used to an audience: "Phoeby's hungry listening helped Janie to tell her story." On this point, Bethel comments that "In presenting Janie's story as a narrative related by herself to her best Black woman friend, Phoeby, Hurston is able to draw upon the rich oral legacy of Black female storytelling and mythmaking that has its roots in Afro-American culture." But this is not an end in itself. Hurston's aim is textuality—the process of producing a text through the transformation of other texts—and through this textuality, a form of feminist self-definition. By transforming Janie's orality—Hurston's intertexts—into textuality, the writer creates both herself as a writer and her own story, while Janie creates her life through language. Creator and character fuse in Hurston's description of Janie's motivation for relating the story that follows: "that oldest human longing—self revelation." All the events of the novel's one long evening find their center in the act of telling the tale.

To understand the effects of the novel's frame, the embodiment of Hurston's narrative strategy, it is useful to suspend consideration of that device for the moment in order first to examine the story Janie tells. The frame consists only of the first chapter and the final three pages of the novel's twentieth and last chapter. Since the story within the story comprises much of the novel, it always commands the greatest critical attention. Here Hurston offers the tale of Janie Crawford's development from puberty to womanhood as a model of black female development. The story begins in the home of her grandmother, moves to the homes of her two husbands, Logan Killicks and then Joe Starks, and concludes with the death of her third husband and lover Vergible "Tea Cake" Woods. Janie orders the story in such a way that she chronicles her progress from dependence to independence, while Hurston gives us the story of Janie's development from silent "object" to speaking "subject."

At the beginning of the story within the story, Janie receives her sense of definition from others. She is woman as object under the control of a racist, patriarchal culture. Failing to recognize herself as the one black child in a photograph, she begins her story without name or color. " 'Dey all useter call me Alphabet 'cause so many people had done named me different names.' " Initially she reconciles herself to the received wisdom, the history of black women's place in the prevailing power structure as imparted by Nanny, her grandmother: " 'Honey, de white man is de ruler of everything as fur as Ah been able tuh find out. Maybe it's some place way off in de ocean where de black man is in power, but we don't know nothin' but what we see. So de white man throw down de load and tell de nigger man tuh pick it up. He pick it up because he have to, but he don't tote it. He hand it to his womenfolks. De nigger woman is de mule uh de world so fur as Ah can see. Ah been prayin' fuh it tuh be different wid you. Lawd, lawd, lawd.' " Nanny projects a stereotypical identity (wife) and a secure future (house and land) for Janie based upon what she knows, which is limited by the historical constraints of what she has seen of the white man's power over blacks and the black man's relationship to the black woman. Thus, she explains to Janie: " 'Ah was born back due in slavery so it wasn't for me to fulfill my dreams of whut a woman oughta be and to do. Dat's one of de hold-backs of slavery.' "

Nanny arranges Janie's marriage to Logan Killicks and his sixty acres of land, thereby "desecrating" Janie's vision from the pear tree of idyllic union. Bethel explains Nanny's behavior as a protective measure: "She is attempting to adjust Janie to the prevailing sexual and racial milieu, and her protectivenes emerges as violence directed against Janie. Nanny attempts to explain to Janie the historical and social forces that make her innocent actions so serious. . . ." Bethel sees in this cross-generational relationship the pattern of black women's victimization by oppressive racial and sexual forces. "In this sense," she concludes, "Janie and her grandmother illustrate the tragic continuity of Black female oppression in white/male America." While it is true that the oppression continues, it is also evident that Hurston makes Janie differ from Nanny in some important ways. Part of what the character learns is to place her grandmother's words in perspective—to understand how Nanny's recounting of experience shaped what Janie was later able to see. In this respect, Hurston stages a break with the oppressor's culture and points to the sexual and racial liberation of women.

The grandmother's gift of a life different from her own permits Janie to pursue dreams and visions beyond those that Nanny, " 'a cracked plate' " damaged by slavery, could have projected. Janie creates her own future, the way to her individual happiness, at the same time that Hurston constructs a new legacy through the tale Janie tells. The story Janie tells Phoeby and the narrative the reader receives are vastly different from the shaping and socializing story Nanny tells Janie. In a sense, Nanny is the unreconstructed past, and Janie her fulfillment through a newly constructed present. Although the grandmother's narrative power has been repressed into further silence, Nanny still envisions the story she longed to tell: " 'Ah wanted to preach a great sermon about colored women sittin' on high, but they wasn't no pulpit for me' "; but silence distorts this story to the point where the horizon of women's potential is constricted to the private sphere of domestic life. Through Janie, Hurston exposes the crack in the plate and preaches the liberating and defiant sermon that Nanny was never able to deliver and that black women, indeed all women, have been waiting to hear. Janie's story can be read as a new (hi)story constructed out of love and passed from one black woman to another.

The process of Janie's freedom from oppressive roles entails several steps and engenders predictable male opposition. Logan Killicks expresses his complaint about Janie's independence in racial terms: " 'You think youse white folks by de way you act.' " Joe Starks brings Janie closer to racial/cultural autonomy by escaping the control of white hegemony. His desire to be a "big voice" in a place beyond the authority of white men suggests change, chance, and the far horizon to Janie, although from the outset she realizes that Starks does not completely embody her vision: "He did not represent sun-up and pollen and blooming trees." From the day she rides off with him in a hired rig, sitting in a seat "like some high, ruling chair," Janie confronts the delimiting structures of language: "Her old thoughts were going to come in handy now, but new words would have to be made and said to fit them." Hers is a new life beyond the limits of the imagined, demanding the creation of a new story for its expression.

Their Eyes Were Watching God is a novel about orality—of speakers and modes of speech: Joe's "big voice" wields power modeled on white culture; the grandmother speaks the language of slavery time; the store porch hosts "mule-talkers" and "big picture talkers"; and each town has its complement of gossips. Here, as everywhere, language produces power and knowledge as well as constraint; it is the ability to interpret and to transform experience. The townspeople perceive the equation of word and law, how Joe's big voice commands obedience: " 'You kin feel a switch in his hand when he's talkin' to yuh' "; " 'he's de wind and we'se de grass. We bend which ever way he blows.' " Commenting on this effect, Howard makes the clever observation that "It is no mistake that he [Joe] often prefaces his remarks with 'I, god.' " Just as the town chorus is alienated by Joe's power of speech, they also note Janie's silence. In this world of lively speakers, Janie lives a speechless existence. At the town's dedication ceremony, Joe speaks when Janie is asked to say a few words. Although he robs her of this opportunity, she sees and reflects upon her loss: "She had never thought of making a speech, and didn't know if she cared to make one at all. It must have been the way Joe spoke out without giving her a chance to say anything one way or another that took the bloom off of things." Janie discovers the emptiness of class status, and especially of status by affiliation—the territory of women. In particular, she grows to understand the loneliness of silence, how orality is required for community. She loves the mule stories people tell on the store porch and creates her own tales in silence, but Joe restricts Janie's personal autonomy by prohibiting her partricipation in discourse. She can neither tell stores nor serve as a member of an audience—the folk community required for the telling.

Through the novel, Hurston also exposes phallocentrism and instructs her readers in the terms of discourse. By means of their oral skills, the porch speakers demonstrate the powerful effects of logocentrism: "They are the center of the world." As in white patriarchal culture, language serves as a locus for social control through its centrality within an order of meaning. Robert Hemenway and Roger Abrahams both comment on the importance of "negotiating respect" through verbal skill in the black community. In "Are You a Flying Lark or a Setting Dove?" Hemenway remarks that "negotiating for respect is not a static process dependent upon the institutions or instrumentalities offered to a woman by society—marriage, the home, the church—but a dynamic response to events growing out of a woman's capacity for self-expression." Phallocentrism is so fundamentally pervasive that it is difficult to conceive of one's self, actions, and meaning outside of its system of control. To attempt to escape its constraints, Janie must use power in order to have power. By transformng her characteristic silence into speech, she stands a chance of establishing a different relationship with Joe, that is, a relationship based on acknowledging difference and accommodating change. Eventually she tires of his endless verbal disputes designed to bring about submission. Her silence in the external world reflects her internal repression until the hollow image of Joe Starks crashes from the shelf in her mind, and she discovers her emotional silence: "She had a host of thoughts she had never expressed to him, and numerous emotions she had never let Jody know about. Things packed up and put away in parts of her heart where he could never find them. She was saving up feelings for some man she had never seen."

The three places in the text where Janie speaks publicly are marked in the novel. When Joe implements Janie's idea by freeing a persecuted mule—

the analogue of black slaves, and especially of black women ("de mule uh de world")—Janie praises him. She gives a speech in which she compares Joe with Abraham Lincoln. The townspeople note her skill: " 'Yo' wife is uh born orator, Starks. Us never knowed dat befo'. She put jus' de right words tuh our thoughts.' " In the second instance, Hurston herself, through the omniscient narrative voice, underscores Janie's incursion into orality: "Janie did what she had never done before, that is, thrust herself into the conversation." This time, instead of presenting an oblique defense of women through the suffering mule, Janie, like Freeman's Sarah Penn and Alice Walker's Celie, gets "too moufy" and preaches her sermon on women (the one Nanny never could deliver) to the men on the porch: " 'Sometimes God gits familiar wid us womenfolks too and talks His inside business. He told me how surprised He was 'bout y'all turning out so smart after Him makin' yuh different; and how surprised y'all is goin' tuh be if you ever find out you don't know half as much 'bout us as you think you do. It's so easy to make yo'self out God Almighty when you ain't got nothin' tuh strain against but women and chickens.' " The final instance of Janie's mastery that ultimately establishes her power occurs when, in retaliation for Joe's verbal abuse, she humiliates him in front of his male friends. She seizes his authority—language—and leaves him speechless.

No unquestioning user of language, Hurston creates her character as a critic of phallocentrism who speaks her defiance. As such, Janie positions herself in a different relation to discourse, moving beyond the exercise of language as a means of establishing power over others or of fixing absolute meaning, to "a practice of language" that Stephen Heath describes as "wild, on the body, unauthorised." Out of pity when Joe is on his death bed, Janie contemplates "what had happened in the making of a voice out of a man." Hélène Cixous's analysis of the politics of language clarifies what Hurston is doing through her character: "No political reflection can dispense with reflection on language, with work on language. For as soon as we exist, we are born into language and language speaks (to) us, dictates its law, a law of death: it lays down its familial model, lays down its conjugal model, and even at the moment of uttering a sentence, admitting a notion of 'being,' a question of being, an ontology, we are already seized by a certain kind of masculine desire, the desire that mobilizes philosophical discourse." Constructing another course for black women, Hurston directs Janie's language toward the discovery of a discourse of emotion, a language she learns through her relationship with Tea Cake who fulfills the bee and blossom imagery of the novel's opening. He demands a union of speech and feeling, and she asks that he speak "with no false pretense." He is the master linguist of "otherness"; as Janie tells Phoeby in the story within the story, " 'So in the beginnin' new thoughts had tuh be thought and new words said. After Ah got used tuh dat, we gits 'long jus' fine. He done taught me de maiden language all over.' " This "maiden" language defies the social construction of difference and permits new perspectives to emerge from narrative action. For example, Janie rejects being "classed off," separated from other black people through her imprisonment in Joe's house and store as "his showpiece, his property." To a degree, she frees herself from his story, another constriction of her horizon, and shares her perception with Phoeby: " 'And Ah'd sit dere wid de walls creepin' up on me and squeezin' all de life outa me.' " Janie rejects the "race after property and titles" in favor of "uh love game." Recognizing that the exclusion of others is the repression of differences within one's self, she merges her life with the life of the black community, telling big stories, listening to them, working along with the other women, and rejecting Mrs. Turner's politics of color—a pecking order that privileges white features over black.

By freeing herself from the oppressor's language and by learning a new integration of words and feeling, Janie develops her critique of color, class, and sex. The narrator, Janie of the retelling, speaks of the repression inherent in Nanny's "mis-love": "Nanny had taken the biggest thing God ever made, the horizon—for no matter how far a person can go the horizon is still way beyond you—and pinched it in to such a little bit of a thing that she could tie it about her granddaughter's neck tight enough to choke her. She hated the old woman who had twisted her so in the name of love." But this recognition becomes Janie's own and is modified by her interpretation of Nanny's circumstance—one can only dream the next dream, and until it is reached, its true value is unknown. Janie explains:

> "She was borned in slavery time when folks, dat is black folks, didn't sit down anytime dey felt lak it. So sittin' on porches lak de white madam looked lak uh mighty fine thing tuh her. Dat's whut she wanted for me—don't keer whut it cost. Git up on uh high chair and sit dere. She didn't have time tuh think whut tuh do after you got up on de stool uh do nothin'. De object wuz tuh git dere. So Ah got up on de high stool lak she told me, but Phoeby, Ah done nearly languished tuh death up dere. Ah felt like de world wuz cryin' extry and Ah ain't read de common news yet."

To a degree Hurston validates Nanny's dream for Janie through Phoeby who, less affluent than her friend, lends sympathy to the grandmother's way of thinking. At the same time, Hurston demonstrates how Nanny's values are the effects produced by the oppressed having internalized the oppressor's consciousness.

Robert Hemenway, commenting on Janie's effort to come to terms with Nanny's vision, maintains that "the vertical metaphor in this speech represents Hurston's entire system of thought, her social and racial philosophy. People erred because they wanted to be *above* others, an impulse which eventually led to denying the humanity of those below. Whites had institutionalized such thinking, and black people were vulnerable to the philosophy because being on high like white folks seemed to represent security and power." In other words, if you haven't had it, power and status look good; so goes the hierarchical dream of the phallocentric economy. Reflecting her commitment to an essential relationship between experience and knowledge, Janie mitigates Tea Cake's regret over his decision not to stay when the hurricane was imminent: " 'When yuh don't know, yuh just don't know.' " She prefers not to trust the projections that, like Nanny's dream for Janie, reproduced the oppressor's logic. In a remarkable way, Hurston wages an early battle on behalf of oppressed people and anticipates black feminist writers such as Audre Lorde. Citing Paulo Freire's *The Pedagogy of the Oppressed,* Lorde proclaims: "The true focus of revolutionary change is never merely the oppressive situations which we seek to escape, but that piece of the oppressor which is planted deep within each of us, and which knows only the oppressor's tactics, the oppressors' relationships." Hurston's effort to supplant the language and logic of this consciousness relates her to radical feminist writers today.

According to Hurston's defiant (deviant) narrative logic, only the Janie of the narrative frame, the one who returns to Eatonville, is capable of telling the story. The voiceless existence of the less experienced Janie prevented narration, except as the story might be presented through a third-person limited or omniscient narrator. This strategy, however, would have diminished the power of Janie's having come to speak, one of the highest forms of acheivement and artistry in the folk community. Thus, Janie's story cannot be told and can only be retold. Surely it is more than my illusion as a white feminist critic that Hurston presents us with a novel of the black woman's struggle to construct a language that destroys the conditions of her historic silence and creates the stories that articulate and make memorable a new (hi)story. Janie can return with an understanding she and Hurston share of the liberating force of language within the black community.

One of Janie's greatest lessons about language centers on its power to deconstruct and to construct, to kill or to give life. When she is on trial for Tea Cake's murder, she recognizes this potential in the black members of the audience: "They were there with their tongues cocked and loaded, the only real weapon left to weak folks. The only killing tool they are allowed to use in the presence of white folks." This passage recalls the frame's opening segment in which Hurston describes the townspeople sitting on their porches at night: "They became lords of sounds and lesser things. They passed nations through their mouths. They sat in judgment." Adopting the traditonal means of defense against gossip, Janie selects Phoeby, a trusted member of the community network, to whom she can provide an account of her behavior. In addition to this pragmatic motive for narration, Janie uses language to give life and memory to feeling. Following the death of the mule, for example, it is memorialized in story by the porch talkers, just as the life of the black woman in slavery is fixed in Nanny's discourse when contrasted with Janie. Thus, according to the conventions of their discursive fields, Janie's story enters oral tradition while Hurston's novel passes into literary tradition. Through her character's discovery, the writer gives us a story of how language outwits time and exclusively patriarchal determinations of meaning, and the reader finds new significance in the frame's opening commentary comparing men, "whose dreams [are] mocked to death by Time," and women: "Now, women forget all those things they don't want to remember, and remember everything they don't want to forget. The dream is the truth. Then they act and do things accordingly."

Although the novel's work is conducted primarily through Janie's story, much of its significance rests in and in relationship to the narrative frame. The importance of the frame is that it permits Hurston to tell her story through a reconstituted subject. Hurston holds to this even at the expense of creating anomalies in Janie's story—the places where Phoeby is mentioned in the third person, dialogues between Phoeby and Janie in which Phoeby is presumably a participant in the telling, since Janie addresses her remarks to her friend. The story we receive is not constituted until Janie returns, changed. She arrives as the witness to a new epistemology: "you got tuh *go* there tuh *know* there." Through Janie's story, Hurston presents an alternative conception of power as it operates in black female discourse. Rather than replicating verbal power as oppression, its form among whites and blacks imitating whites, Hurston espouses a form of narrative authority indigenous to black tribal tradition. As Ruth Borker notes of the Buhaya of Tanzania, "The key cultural concept for thinking about speech is that of 'knowing.' " Janie operates according to a system whereby you don't say what you don't know, and you can't know something until you experience it; or, as Jacques Derrida puts it, "the logocentrist or logocentric impulse is rocked by historical events, rocked by things that happen." Having gone there, you are changed, and the story you have to tell is a different stotry. The interpretations of the phallocentric hegemony are called into question rather than assumed. This move wrests the control of meaning from a sexist, racist culture and locates the potential for change within the individual.

Besides the significance of how the story is changed by the fact that Janie has gone and returned, it is additionally important that Janie returns as a "speaking subject" to bring her story to the people. At this point, the changed Janie, Janie the storyteller, fuses with the author. Hurston designates the end of Janie's story with the novel's only authentic silence—one that is elected rather than imposed, and is as natural as the sounds that mark the ending: "There was a finished silence after that so that for the first time they could hear the wind picking at the pine trees." With the full resonance of the parallel, *Their Eyes Were Watching God* might well be understood as a "Portrait of the Artist as a Black Woman."

Through the overarching and elusive meaning of her title, Hurston confronts the dilemma of the phallocentric ground of determinate meaning. At the most critical moments in the novel, Janie and others scrutinize the heavens for a sign of God's intention. Like their African ancestors (and the Puritan interpreters), they are seeking a way through nature to unlock and interpret the meaning of events. They act out the reader's effort to interpret the text. In the novel's opening frame, we encounter the Watcher, an Everyman waiting for the ship of dreams to come in and trying to outwit Death who was "there before there was a where or a when or a then." Following Janie's sensual awakening, she desires validation for her dreams: "She was seeking confirmation of the voice and vision, and everywhere she found and acknowledged answers. A personal answer for all other creations except herself. She felt an answer seeking her, but where? When? How?" Only once does there seem to be a sign—the arrival of Tea Cake, which Janie invests with referential power taking us back to the blossoming pear tree and the bee: "He looked like the love thoughts of women. He could be a bee to a blossom—a pear tree blossom in the spring. He seemed to be crushing scent out of the world with his footsteps. Crushing aromatic herbs with every step he took. Spices hung about him. He was a glance from God."

While Janie accepts Tea Cake as a sign, his presence cannot resolve the problem of interpretation—the signification of events. When the hurricane is imminent, people consider God's purpose: "They sat in company with the others in other shanties, their eyes straining against crude walls and their souls asking if He meant to measure their puny might against His. They seemed to be staring at the dark, but their eyes were watching God." The only answer given is the storm itself, suggesting that the people's question, as related by the narrator, contained its answer, that this was indeed a contest of force. The hurricane and Tea Cake's love for Janie ultimately contribute to his death, so that on a symbolic level, it would seem that what was once responsible for his presence is in the end responsible for his absence. Through the compelling imagery of the frame, Hurston refuses this simple dichotomy by rejecting the bipolar logic of absence: "Tea Cake, with the sun for a shawl. Of course he wasn't dead. He could never be dead until she herself had finished feeling and thinking. The kiss of his memory made pictures of love and light against the wall. Here was peace. She pulled in her horizon like a great fish-net. Pulled it from around the waist of the world and draped it over her shoulder. So much of life in its meshes! She called in her soul to come and see." The effect Derrida describes in approaching Sollers' *Numbers* expands our sense of Hurston's accomplishment here: "The text is out of sight when it compels the horizon itself to enter the frame of its own scene, so as to 'learn to embrace with increased grandeur the horizon of the present time.'" Through Janie's exemplary insistence on a different (black and female) determination of meaning and value, and through her own narrative art as the teller within the tale, Hurston resists the binary opposition of phallocentrism as it inhabits Western metaphysics, just as she seeks to revise its attendant notion of interpretation. The present, as an unexperienced future, cannot unlock the meaning of what is to come. It has no predictive or determinative value.

In place of this practice, Hurston offers a particular concept of presence—the presence of a present—through Janie's retelling. The only present is its illusion in narration, occasioned by and filling in for absence. Bringing the past into the present, Hurston gives both dimensions a particular reconstructed value, and propels the past, itself a former present, toward a future that exists only as an anticipated possibility for black women. Thus, these elements of time remain fluid, each containing traces of the other. As storytellers, as speaking subjects, Janie and Hurston don't escape phallocentrism. Rather, they stage a critique from what Derrida calls "a certain inside of logocentrism. But it is an inside that is divided enough and tormented enough and obsessed enough by the other, by contradictions, by heterogeneity, for us to be able to say things about it without being simply 'outside of it.' And we say them within the grammar, within the language of logocentrism while allowing the alterity or the difference which obsesses this inside to show through." By extricating herself from cultural control, Janie/Hurston creates culture. Through the retelling of Janie's story, orality becomes textuality. Textuality is produced by Janie's learned orality, her participation in the oral tradition of the culture. She learns to be one of the people; thus, this is a story of her acculturation into black womanhood and her artistic entitlement to language. By chronicling Janie's development, Hurston transforms the status of narrative from the temporality characteristic of oral traditon to the more enduring textuality required to outwit time's effect on memory. In doing so, she presents feminist readers with a map of a woman's personal resistance to patriarchy, and feminist writers—in particular Alice Walker—with the intertext for later feminist works.

A Black and Idiomatic Free Indirect Discourse

Barbara Johnson and Henry Louis Gates, Jr.

Hurston's use of free indirect discourse is central to her larger strategy of critiquing what we might think of as a "male writing." Joe Starks, we remember, fondly and unconsciously refers to himself as "I-God." During the lamp-lighting ceremony, as we have suggested earlier, Joe is represented as the creator (or at least the purchaser) of light. Joe is the text's figure of authority and voice, indeed the authority *of* voice:

> "Naw, Jody, it jus' looks lak it keeps us in some way we ain't natural wid one 'nother. You'se always off talkin' and fixin' things, and Ah feels lak Ah'm jus' markin' time. Hope it soon gits over."
>
> "Over, Janie? I god, Ah ain't even started good. Ah told you in de very first beginnin' dat Ah aimed tuh be uh big voice. You oughta be glad, 'cause dat makes uh big woman outa you."

Joe says that "in de very first beginnin' " that he "aimed tuh be uh big voice," an echo of the first verse of the Gospel according to Saint John:

> In the beginning was the Word, and the Word was with God, and the Word was God.

Joe, we know, sees himself, and wishes to be seen as the God-figure of his community. The text tells us that when speakers on formal occasions prefaced their remarks with the phrase, "Our beloved Mayor," the phrase was

---

From *Reading Zora: Discourse and Rhetoric in* Their Eyes Were Watching God. © 1987 by Henry Louis Gates, Jr. and Barbara Johnson. Methuen and Co., 1987

equivalent to "one of those statements that everybody says but nobody believes like 'God is everywhere.' " Joe is the figure of the male author, he who has "authored" both Eatonville and Janie's existences. We remember that when Joe lights the town's newly acquired lamp, Mrs. Bogle's alto voice sings "Jesus, the Light of the World":

> We walk in de light, de beautiful light
> Come where the dew drops of mercy shine bright.
> Shine all around us by day and by night
> Jesus, the light of the world.

So, when Janie Signifies upon Joe, telling him that he not only is nothing but a man, but is an *impotent* man at that, the revelation of the truth *kills* him.

Janie, in effect, has *rewritten* Joe's text of himself, and liberated herself in the process. Janie "writes" herself into being by *naming,* by speaking herself free. In *The Color Purple,* Alice Walker takes this moment in Hurston's text as the moment of revision, and creates a character whom we witness literally writing herself into being, but writing herself into being in a language that imitates that idiom *spoken* by Janie and Hurston's black community generally. This scene and this transformation or reversal of status is truly the first feminist critique of the fiction of the authority of the male voice, and its sexism, in the Afro-American tradition.

It is prefigured, perhaps, in Hurston's subtle revision of Douglass's well-known apostrophe in the opening two paragraphs of *Their Eyes.* Hurston underscores her revision of Douglass's canonical text by using two chiasmuses in her opening paragraphs. As Ephi Paul argues convincingly, the subject of the second paragraph of *Their Eyes Were Watching God* ("women") reverses the subject of the first ("men") and figures the nature of their respective desire in opposite terms: a man's desire becomes reified into a disappearing ship, and he is transformed from a human being into "a Watcher," his desire personified onto an object, beyond his grasp or control, external to himself. Nanny, significantly, uses this "male" figure ("Ah, could see uh big ship at a distance") as does Tea Cake, whose use *reverses* Douglass's by indicating Tea Cake's claim of control of his fate and capacity to satisfy Janie's desire: "Can't no ole man stop me from gittin' no ship for yuh if dat's what you want. Ah'd git dat ship out from under him so slick til he'd be walkin' de water lak ole Peter befo' he knowed it."

A woman, by contrast, represents desire metaphorically, Paul argues, rather than metonymically, by controlling the process of *memory,* an active subjective process figured in the pun on (re)membering, as in the process of narration which Janie will share with her friend, Phoeby, which we shall "overhear." For a woman, "The dream is the truth," the truth is her dream. Janie, as we shall see, is thought to be (and is maintained) "inarticulate" by her first two husbands, but is a master of metaphorical narration; Joe Starks, her most oppressive husband, by contrast, is a master of metonym, an opposition which Janie must navigate her selves through to achieve self-knowledge. Its first sentence ("Now, women forget all those things they don't want to remember, and remember everything they don't want to forget") is itself a chiasmus (women/remember//remember/forget), echoing the structure of Douglass's famous chiasmus ("You have seen how a man became a slave, you will see how a slave became a man"). Indeed, Douglass's major contribution to the slave's narrative was to make chiasmus the central trope of slave narration, in which a slave-object writes him- or herself into a human-subject through the act of writing. The overarching rhetorical strategy of the slave narratives written after 1845 can be represented as a chiasmus, as repetition and reversal. Hurston, in these enigmatic opening paragraphs, Signifies upon Douglass through formal revision, and creates a well-defined space for a woman's narrative voice in a male-determined tradition.

If *Their Eyes* makes impressive use of the figures of outside and inside, as well as the metaphor of double-consciousness as the prerequisite to becoming a speaking subject, then the text's mode of narration, especially its "speakerlyness," serves as the rhetorical analogue to this theme. We use the word "double" here intentionally, both to echo W. E. B. Du Bois's trope for the Afro-American's peculiar psychology of citizenship and to avoid the limited description of free indirect discourse as a "dual voice," in Roy Pascal's term. Rather than a "dual voice," as it were, free indirect discourse, as manifested in *Their Eyes Were Watching God,* is a dramatic way of expressing a *divided* self. Janie's self, as we have seen, is a divided self. Long before she becomes aware of her division, of her "inside" and "outside," free indirect discourse communicates this division to the reader. After she becomes aware of her own division, free indirect discourse functions to represent, rhetorically, her *interrupted* passage from "outside" to "inside." Free indirect discourse, furthermore, is a central aspect of the rhetoric of the text, and serves to disrupt the reader's expectation of the necessity of the shift in point of view from third person to first within Janie's framed narrative. Free indirect discourse is not the "voice" of *both* a character *and* a narrator; rather, it is a bivocal utterance, containing elements of both direct and indirect speech. It is an "utterance" that no one could have spoken, yet which we recognize because of its characteristic "speakerly-ness," its paradoxically *written* manifestation of the aspiration to the *oral*.

We shall not enter into the terminological controversy over free indirect discourse; our concern with this topic is limited to its use in *Their Eyes*. We are especially interested in its presence in this text as an implicit critique of that ancient opposition in narrative theory between "showing" and "telling," between *mimesis* and *diegesis*. The tension between *diegesis,* understood here as that which can be represented, and *mimesis,* that which Hurston "repeats," as it were, in direct quotations, strikes the reader early on as a fundamental opposition in *Their Eyes*. Only actions or events can be represented, in this sense, while discourse, here, would seem to be "overheard" or "repeated." Hurston's use of this form of repetition creates the illusion of a direct relation between her text and a black "real world" (which has led some of her most vocal critics to call this an "anthropological" text), while representation of the sort found in narrative commentary preserves, even insists upon, the difference and the very distance between them.

Free indirect discourse, on the other hand, is a third, mediating term. As Michael Ginsberg argues perceptively, "it is a *mimesis* which tries to pass for a *diegesis*." But it is also, we contend, a *diegesis* that tries to pass for a *mimesis*. Indeed, it is precisely this understanding of free indirect discourse that derives from its usages in *Their Eyes Were Watching God,* simply because we are unable to characterize it either as the representation of an action (*diegesis*) or as the repetition of a character's words (*mimesis*). When we recall Hurston's insistence that the fundamental indicator of traditional black oral narration is its aspiration to the *dramatic* (her term), we can see clearly that her use of free indirect discourse is a profound attempt to *remove* the distinction between repeated "speech" and represented events. Here, discourse "is not distinct from events." As Ginsberg argues, "Subject and object dissolve into each other. Representation which guaranteed the distance between them is in danger." For Hurston, free indirect discourse is an equation: direct speech equals narrative commentary; representation of an action equals repetition of that action; therefore, narrative commentary aspires to the immediacy of the drama. Janie's quest for consciousness, however, always remains that of the consciousness of her own division, which the dialogical rhetoric of the text—especially as expressed in free indirect discourse—underscores, preserves, and seems to celebrate. It is this theme, and this rhetoric of division, which together comprise the "modernism" of this text.

A convenient way to think about free indirect discourse is that it appears, initially, to be indirect discourse (by which we mean that its signals of time and person correspond to a third-person narrator's discourse) "but it is penetrated, in its syntactic and semantic structures, by enunciative properties, thus by the discourse of a character," as Ginsberg argues, and even in Hurston's case, by that of characters. In other words, free indirect discourse attempts to represent "consciousness without the apparent intrusion of a narrative voice," thereby "presenting the illusion of a character's acting out his [or her] mental state in an immediate relationship with the reader." Graham Hough defines free indirect discourse as one extreme of "coloured narrative," or narrative-cum-dialogue as in Jane Austen's fictions. Hurston's use of free indirect discourse, we are free to say, is indeed a kind of colored narrative! But Hurston allows us to rename free indirect discourse; near the beginning of her book, the narrator describes the communal, undifferentiated voice of "the porch" as "A mood come alive. Words walking without masters; walking together like harmony in a song." Since the narrator attributes these words to "the bander log," or the place where Kipling's monkeys sit, Hurston here gives one more, coded, reference to Signifyin(g): that which "the porch" (monkeys) has just done is to Signify upon Janie. It Signifyin(g) is "a mood come alive," "words walking without masters," then we can also think of free indirect discourse in this way.

There are numerous indices whereby we identify free indirect discourse in general, among these grammar, intonation, context, idiom, register, content; it is naturalized in a text by stream of consciousness, irony, empathy, and polyvocality. The principal indices of free indirect discourse in *Their Eyes* include those which "evoke a 'voice' or presence" that supplements the narrator's, especially when one or more sentences of free indirect discourse follow a sentence of indirect discourse. Idiom and register, particularly, Hurston uses as markers of black colloquialism, to create the "speakerly" aspect of even the narrator's commentary, informed by the dialect of the direct discourse of the black characters. In *Their Eyes*, naturalization would seem to function as part of the theme of the developing, but discontinuous, self. This function is naturalized primarily by irony, empathy, and polyvocality. When it is used in conjunction with Joe Starks, irony obtains and distancing results; when it is used in conjunction with Janie, empathy obtains and illusory identification results, an identity that we might call "lyric fusion" between the narrator and Janie. Bivocalism, finally, or the "double-voiced" utterance, in which two voices co-occur, is this text's central device of naturalization, again serving to reinforce both

Janie's division and, paradoxically, the narrator's distance from Janie. As Ginsberg concludes so perceptively, "Free indirect discourse is a way of expression of a divided self."

Their Eyes employs three modes of narration to render the words or thoughts of a character. The first is direct discourse:

> "Jody," she smiled up at him, "but s'posin—"
> "Leave de s'posin' and everything else to me."

The next is indirect discourse:

> The vision of Logan Killicks was desecrating the pear tree, but Janie didn't know how to tell Nanny that.

The third example is free indirect discourse. Significantly, this example occurs when Joe Starks enters the narrative:

> Joe Starks was the man, yeah Joe Starks from in and through Georgy. Been workin' for white folks all his life. Saved up some money—round three hundred dollars, yes indeed, right *here* in his pocket. Kept hearin' 'bout them buildin' a new state down heah in Floridy and sort of wanted to come. But he was makin' money where he was. But when he heard all about 'em makin' a town all outa colored folks, he knowed dat was de place he wanted to be. He had always wanted to be a big voice, but de white folks had all de sayso where he come from and everywhere else, exceptin' dis place dat colored folks was buildin' theirselves. Dat was right too. De man dat built things oughta boss it. Let colored folks build things too if dey wants to crow over somethin'. He was glad he had his money all saved up. He meant to git here whilst de town wuz yet a baby. He meant to buy in big (emphasis added).

We selected this example because it includes a number of standard indices of free indirect speech. Although when read aloud, it sounds as if entire sections are in, or should be in, direct quotation, none of the sentences in the paragraph are direct discourse. There are no quotation marks here. The character's idiom, interspersed and contrasted colorfully with the narrator's voice, indicates nevertheless that this is an account of the words that Joe spoke to Janie. The sentences imitating dialect clearly are not those of the narrator alone; they are those of Joe Sparks *and* the narrator. Moreover, the presence of the adverb *here* ("yes, indeed, right here in his pocket") as opposed to "there," which would be required in normal indirect speech because one source would be describing another, informs us that the assertion originates within and reflects the character's sensibilities, not the narrator's. The interspersion of indirect discourse with free indirect discourse, even in the same sentence, serves as another index to its presence, precisely by underscoring Joe's characteristic idiom, whereas the indirect discourse obliterates it. Despite the third person and the past tense, then, of which both indirect and free indirect discourse consist, several sentences in this paragraph appear to *report* Joe's speech, without the text resorting to either dialogue or direct discourse. The principal indices of free indirect discourse direct the reader to the subjective source of the statement, rendered through a fusion of narrator and a "silent" but "speaking" character.

Exclamations and exclamatory questions often introduce free indirect discourse. The text's first few examples occur when Janie experiences the longing for love, and then her first orgasm:

> She saw a dust-bearing bee sink into the sanctum of a bloom; the thousand sister-calyxes arch to meet the love embrace and the ecstatic shiver of the tree from root to tiniest branch creaming in every blossom and frothing with delight. So this was a marriage! . . . Then Janie felt a pain remorseless sweet that left her limp and lanquid.

Then, in the next paragraph:

> She was lying across the bed asleep so Janie tipped on out of the front door. Oh to be a pear tree—*any* tree in bloom! With kissing bees singing of the beginning of the world! She was sixteen.

Unlike the free indirect discourse that introduces Joe, these three sentences retain the narrator's level of diction, her idiom, as if to emphasize, on one hand, that Janie represents the *potentially* lyrical self, but on the other hand, that the narrator is "interpreting" Janie's *inarticulate* thoughts to the reader on her behalf.

This usage remains fairly consistent until Janie begins to challenge, if only in her thoughts, Joe's authority:

> Janie noted that while he didn't talk the mule himself [Signify], he sat and laughed at it. But then when Lige or Sam or Walter or some of the other big picture talkers were using a side of the world for a canvas, Joe would hustle her off inside the store to sell something. Look like he took pleasure in doing it. Why couldn't he go himself sometimes? She had come to hate the inside of that store anyway.

Here we see Janie's idiom entering, if only in two sentences, the free indirect speech. After she has "slain" Jody, however, her idiom, more and more, informs the free indirect discourse, in sentences such as "Poor Jody! He ought not to have to wrassle in there by himself." Once Janie meets Tea Cake, the reader comes to expect to encounter Janie's doubts and dreams in free indirect discourse, almost always introduced by the narrator explicitly as being Janie's thoughts. Almost never, curiously enough, does Janie's free indirect discourse unfold in a strictly black idiom, as does Joe's; rather, it is represented in an idiom *informed* by the black idiom but translated into what we might think of as a colloquial form of standard English, which always stands in contrast to Janie's direct speech, which is always foregrounded in dialect.

This difference between the representations of the level of diction of Janie's discourse and the free indirect discourse that the text asks us to accept as the figure of Janie's thoughts, reinforces for the reader both Janie's divided consciousness as well as the double-voiced nature of free indirect discourse, as if the narrative commentary cannot relinquish its proprietary consciousness over Janie as freely as it does for other characters. Nevertheless, after Janie falls in love with Tea Cake, we learn of her feelings through a remarkable amount of free indirect discourse, almost always rendered in what we wish to call "idiomatic," but standard, English.

It is this same voice, eventually, which we also come to associate with that of the text's narrator; with empathy and irony, the narrator begins to "read" Janie's world and everyone in it, using this same rhetorical device, rendered in this identical diction, even when the observation clearly is not Janie's. The effect is as if the lyrical language created by the indeterminate merging of the narrator's voice and Janie's almost totally silences the initial level of diction of the narrator's voice. Let us recall the narrator's voice in the text's opening paragraph:

> Ships at a distance have every man's wish on board. For some they come in with the tide. For others they sail forever on the horizon, never out of sight, never landing until the Watcher turns his eyes away in resignation, his dreams mocked to death by Time. That is the life of men.

Compare that voice with the following:

> So Janie began to think of Death. Death, that strange being with the huge square toes who lived way in the West. The great one who lived in the straight house like a platform without sides to

it, and without a cover. What need has Death for a cover, and what winds can blow against him?

Ostensibly, these are Janie's thoughts. But compare this sentence, which is part of the narrator's commentary: "But, don't care how firm your determination is, you can't keep turning round in one place like a horse grinding sugar cane." Clearly, this is not Janie's discourse, yet the idiom of the sentence is "vernacular-informed."

This idiomatic voice narrates almost completely the dramatic scene of the hurricane, where "six eyes were questioning *God*." One such passage serves as an excellent example of a *communal* free indirect discourse, of a narrative voice that is not fused with Janie's, but which describes events in the *idiom* of "Janie's" free indirect discourse:

> They looked back. Saw people trying to run in raging waters and screaming when they found they couldn't. A huge barrier of the makings of the dike to which the cabins had been added was rolling tumbling forward. . . . The monstropolous beast had left his bed. . . . The sea was walking the earth with a heavy heal.

In several passages after this narration of the hurricane, the interspersed indirect discourse and free indirect discourse become extraordinarily difficult to isolate, because of this similarity in idiom. The text reads:

> Janie fooled around outside awhile to try and think it wasn't so. . . . Well, she thought, that big old dawg with the hatred in his eyes had killed her after all. She wished she had slipped off that cow-tail and drowned then and there and been done. But to kill her through Tea Cake was too much to bear. Tea Cake, the son of the Evening Sun, had to die for loving her. She looked hard at the sky for a long time. Somewhere up there beyond blue ether's bottom sat He. Was He noticing what was going on around here? . . . Did he *mean* to do this thing to Tea Cake and her? . . . Maybe it was some big tease and when he saw it had gone far enough He'd give her a sign.

Narrative commentary and free indirect discourse, in passages such as this, move toward the indistinguishable. The final instance of free indirect discourse occurs, appropriately enough, in the novel's ultimate paragraph, in which Janie's true figurative synthesis occurs:

> The day of the gun, and the bloody body, and the courthouse came and commenced to sing a sobbing sigh out of every corner

in the room; out of each and every chair and thing. Commenced
to sing, commenced to sob and sing, singing and sobbing. Then
Tea Cake came prancing around her where she was and the song
of the sigh flew out of the window and lit in the top of the pine
trees. Tea Cake, with the sun for a shawl. Of course he wasn't
dead. He could never be dead until she herself had finished feeling
and thinking. The kiss of his memory made pictures of love and
light against the wall. Here was peace. She pulled in her horizon
like a great fish-net. Pulled it from around the waist of the world
and draped it over her shoulder. So much of life in its meshes!
She called in her soul to come and see.

Paul, in a subtle reading of various tropes in *Their Eyes,* argues that
this "final moment of transcendence" is also a final moment of control and
synthesis of the opposed "male" and "female" paradigmatic tropes defined
in the novel's first two paragraphs, to which we alluded earlier:

> The horizon that she learns about from Joe, that helps her re-
> discover how to "play" again with Tea Cake, has been trans-
> formed from the object of a longing gaze to a figurative "fish-
> net" which an active subject can pull in. While Joe's desires are,
> like the men of the first paragraph, "mocked to death by Time,"
> Janie's are still alive and thriving: "The kiss of his memory made
> pictures of love and light against the wall." Janie finds "peace"
> in "his memory," just as she has always privileged her inward
> contemplative self over the outer active one. Yet in its own way,
> Janie's thriving survival of hard times has been an active process
> of finding a language to name her desire. The horizon as a fish-
> net seems to signify the synthesis of "men" and "women's"
> figuration, because the fish-net's "meshes" seem so like the sift-
> ing of women's memories—remembering and forgetting all that
> they want. So Janie has cast her horizon into a sea of possibilities
> and sorted out her catch of loves, naming them with an even
> more accurate figuration of desire. She opens her arms to "the
> waist of the world" and gathers in her satisfactions, rooted in
> her power of "feeling and thinking" for herself.

This merging of the opposed modes of figuration in the novel's first two
paragraphs stands as an analogue of Janie's transcendent moment because,
as Paul argues,

> the male and female modes of figuration (as established in the
> "paradigm" of its first two paragraphs)—bring together the ho-

rizon of change and the fish-net of memory. In her search for desire and its naming, Janie shifts back and forth between the alienation of the gazing "Watcher" and the empowerment of women believing that "the dream is the truth." She finds her satisfaction only after using Joe's horizon of "change and chance" to transform the desire she experiences alone under the pear tree; she retains the horizon long after she has dismissed Joe, because she can re-figure to have meaning for herself.

To this we would add that both the "pullin *in*" of "her horizon" and the calling "in" of "her soul" reveal not a unit of self, but a maximum of self-control over the division between self and other. Whereas, before Tea Cake, Janie was forced to send a mask of herself *outward,* now, at the novel's end, she can invite both "her horizon" (the figure for her desires after meeting Jody) and "her soul" inside of herself "to come and see." She has internalized her metaphors, and brought them home, across a threshold heretofore impenetrable. This self-willed, active, subjective synthesis is a remarkable trope of self-knowledge. And the numerous sentences of free indirect discourse in this paragraph serve to stress this fact of Janie's self-knowledge and self-control. Her invitation to her soul to come see the "horizon" that had always before been a figure for external desire, the desire of the other, is the novel's sign of Janie's synthesis.

It is because of these dramatic shifts in the idiom in which the voice of the narrator appears, that we might think that *Their Eyes* as a "speakerly" text. For it is clear that the resonant dialect of the character's discourse has come to "color" the narrator's idiom such that it resembles rather closely the idiom in which Janie's free indirect discourse is rendered. But *Their Eyes* would seem to be a speakerly text for still another reason. Hurston uses free indirect discourse to represent not only an individual character's speech and thought, but also the *collective* black community's speech and thoughts, as in the hurricane passage above. This sort of anonymous, collective, free indirect discourse is not only unusual, but quite possibly was Hurston's innovation. It serves to emphasize both the immense potential of this literary diction, one "dialect-informed," as it were, for the tradition, as well as the text's apparent aspiration to imitate oral narration. One example follows:

> Most of the flame-throwers were there and naturally, handling Big John de Conquer and his works. How he had done everything big on earth, then went up tuh heben without dying atall. Went up there picking a guitar and got all de angels doing the

> ring-shout round and round de throne . . . that brought them
> back to Tea Cake. How come he couldn't hit that box a lick or
> two? Well, all right now, make us know it.

Still another example is even more telling:

> Everybody was talking about it that night. But nobody was
> worried. The fire dance kept up till nearly dawn. The next day,
> more Indians moved east, unhurried but steady. Still a blue sky
> and fair weather. Beans running fine and prices good, so the
> Indians could be, *must* be, wrong. You couldn't have a hurricane
> when you're making seven and eight dollars a day picking beans.
> Indians are dumb anyhow, always were. Another night of Stew
> Beef making dynamic subtleties with his drum and living, sculp-
> tural, grotesques in the dance.

These instances of free indirect discourse are followed in the text by straight
diegesis, which retains the dialect-informed echoes of the previous passage:

> Morning came without motion. The winds, to the tiniest, lisping
> baby breath had left the earth. Even before the sun gave light,
> dead day was creeping from bush to bush watching man.

There are many other examples of this curious voice. Hurston, in this
innovation, is asserting that an entire narration could be rendered if not in
"dialect," then in a dialect-informed discourse. This form of collective,
impersonal free indirect discourse echoes Hurston's definition of "a mood
come alive. Words walking without masters; walking together like harmony in a song." The ultimate sign of the dignity and strength of the black
voice is this use of a dialect-informed free indirect discourse as narrative
commentary beyond that which represents Janie's thoughts and feelings
alone.

There are paradoxes and ironies in speakerly texts. The irony of this
dialect-informed diction, of course, is that it is not a repetition of a language
that anyone speaks; indeed, it can never be spoken. As several other scholars
of free indirect discourse have argued, free indirect discourse is "speaker-
less," by which they mean "the presentation of a perspective outside the
normal communication paradigm that usually characterizes language." It
is literary language, meant to be read in a text. Its paradox is that it comes
into use by Hurston so that discourse rendered through direct, indirect, or
free indirect means may partake of Hurston's "word pictures," and
"thought pictures," as we recall she defined the nature of Afro-American

spoken language. "The white man thinks in a written language," she argued, "and the Negro thinks in hieroglyphics." The speakerly diction of *Their Eyes* attempts to render these pictures through the imitation of the extensively metaphorical medium of black speech, in an oxymoronic "oral hieroglyphic" that is meant only for the printed page. Its obvious oral base, nevertheless, suggests that Hurston conceived of it as a third language, as a mediating third term that aspires to resolve the tension between standard English and black vernacular, just as the narrative device of free indirect discourse aspires to define the traditional opposition between *mimesis* and *diegesis* as a false opposition. And perhaps this dialogical diction, and this dialogical narrative device, can serve as a metaphor for the critic of black comparative literature whose theoretical endeavor is intentially double-voiced as well.

"Mah Tongue Is in Mah Friend's Mouf": The Rhetoric of Intimacy and Immensity in *Their Eyes Were Watching God*

John F. Callahan

The call-and-response tradition of storytelling is the inspiration, instrumental form for Zora Neale Hurston's *Their Eyes Were Watching God*. Hurston grew up inside the oral tradition of the South. As a girl in the all-black town of Eatonville, Florida, she relished the repartee between the men gathered on the porch of Joe Clarke's store and the women passing in and out. What she "really loved to hear was the menfolks holding a 'lying session.' " From them she heard tales of the Creation and the animal stories of Br'er Rabbit and Br'er Fox, Sis Cat and Sis Goose. And sometimes black women told folktales. Hurston first heard the story of color—God's "Git back!" misunderstood as "Git black!"—wonderfully embellished by Gold, a new woman in town and a bold enough performer to come forward in public as a storyteller.

At a young age Hurston had visions and began to make up "little stories." She told stories to her mother and, though her interfering grandmother urged that she be whipped for her "lying tongue," her mother "never tried to break" her. Her mother was an open but unindulgent audience. "She'd listen sometimes, and sometimes she wouldn't. But she never seemed displeased." As her daughter's primary early audience, Lucy Hurston sensed the girl's extraordinary power of voice. On her deathbed she gave Zora "solemn instructions that no one was to take a pillow from under her head as she was dying, and neither the clock nor the looking glass in the room was to be covered with cloth." "She depended on me for voice," Hurston wrote later of her mother's reliance on her as the only one willing to defy the townspeople's folk customs and honor her wish to die like an individual. At the time no one listened. Her father forcibly restrained her, and Hurston grew up feeling the double burden of her mother's trust and reproach because she had failed to make her voice an instrument of action and change in the local world of Eatonville.

In her autobiography Huston also acknowledges her later struggle for voice as a writer. *Their Eyes Were Watching God* "was dammed up in me, and I wrote it under internal pressure in seven weeks. I wish that I could write it again," she confesses implying that, like spoken tales, stories told on paper are not necessarily final. Those who hear or read a story, including sometimes its author, complete and also continue it by virtue of their response. Intriguingly, in view of the collaborative artifice at work in *Their Eyes Were Watching God,* Hurston testifies to the presence of a call from outside as well as from within. "Anyway," she declares, "the force from somewhere in Space which commands you to write in the first place, gives you no choice. You take up the pen when you are told, and write what is commanded." Hurston's observations reinforce *Their Eyes Were Watching God*'s thematic fusion of intimacy and immensity, personal and impersonal reality; her words also direct attention to the novel's fusion of individual and collaborative narrative authority as adapted from the call and response of oral storytelling. In *Their Eyes Were Watching God* Hurston's voice is the lead voice. She performs with her characters, autonomously and separately yet collaboratively, in an asymmetrical relation reminiscent of the poly-rhythms of African music and early African-American antiphonal songs. Hurston imbues her voice with the narrative identity and personality as-sociated with oral storytellers who performed and embellished the stories they told. Through a double act of storytelling and narrative, Hurston calls readers to respond to Janie Crawford's story and her novel with "new thoughts" and "new words."

In my immediate act of reading I was a friend to the novel. I flowed with its story, lived in its world, listened to its voices. I was audience to Hurston and Janie simultaneously. And I felt like a participant about to break into my own voice and continue the story. But afterward, like Janie, I had to overcome other voices, in my case voices of scholarly authority, before I could listen to my own. For a while, under the influence of Robert Stepto, a critic vitally concerned with "authorial control" as an agent in the African-American "quest for freedom and literacy," I questioned my response. To him, "the one great flaw in *Their Eyes*" was the use of third-person point of view. He imagines that Hurston's "curious insistence on having Janie's tale—her personal history in and as a literary form—told by an omniscient third person, rather than by a first-person narrator, implies that Janie has not really won her voice and self after all—that her author (who is quite likely the omniscient narrating voice) cannot see her way clear to giving Janie her voice outright." But eventually I realized that Hurston, always eclectic, original, idiosyncratic, individual, experimental, had decided to challenge the once innovative and generative but by the mid-thirties increasingly pat and closed modernist position against fraternization between novelist and character. I realized that in a personal way Hurston's form asks readers to trust their voices, and that to trust her voice I had to trust my own.

Their Eyes Were Watching God is Hurston's novelistic Emancipation Proclamation as earlier *Mules and Men* had been her Declaration of Independence from the conventions of anthropology. In *Mules and Men* Hurston applied to anthropology an insight about perception and perspective going back at least to Henry James. She realized, in ways her precursors and many successors have not, that her method of observation and manner of self-presentation influenced the people's (or subjects') expression and revelation of their culture. So she abandoned the premise of impersonal, third-person scholarly objectivity, and made *Mules and Men* into a first-person story about her initiation into the practice of fieldwork as well as a collection of the tales she gathered. She became a character in *Mules and Men* as she had been a participant in the black communities of Eatonville and Polk County. Her experience of Negro folklore as "not a thing of the past" but part of a culture "still in the making" mediates between her story and the tales told by her "subjects." Her slowly developing relationships with the people under study and theirs with her authenticate *Mules and Men* both as anthropology and as an autobiographical tale.

Mules and Men establishes Hurston's familiarity with the possibilities of first-person narration as well as with the ambiguous implications of the so-called third-person omniscient voice; i. e., what voice, however impersonal in tone or objective in method, can be all-knowing in the face of reality's chaos and contingency? In *Their Eyes Were Watching God* Hurston breathes into her third-person narration the living voice of a storyteller. Implicitly, she puts her personality on the line. For the fashionable value of authorial control she substitutes a rhetoric of intimacy developed from the collaborative habit of call and response. Moreover, her performance gives the impression that she is embellishing a story she's heard before, if not from Janie, perhaps from Pheoby, Janie's immediate, responsive audience. Because of her intimate yet impersonal form, Hurston invites her readers to respond as listeners and participants in the work of storytelling.

II

Like Janie Crawford's self-presentation as an autonomous black woman simultaneously in and against the Eatonville grain, Hurston's narrative is deliberately anomalous. Authorial control implies a struggle for the story among two or more different voices, analogous to the spirit of competition which sometimes animates oral storytelling. But the two major voices in *Their Eyes Were Watching God* do not contend; rather, they cooperate and collaborate. For Hurston's novel tells the story of a black woman's struggle to chart her life and choose the tones of her voice—a quest familiar to Hurston. And Janie first masters, then seeks to transcend the tradition of verbal contest. For her and for Hurston, storytelling and narrative lead to an intimate mutual response. Each seeks to overcome the jarring distraction of narrow competitive voices with a lyrical serenity subtly keyed to liberation, autonomy, and, finally, honest reciprocal contact. The shared rhetorical space of *Their Eyes Were Watching God* leads to the fusing of Janie's silent interior consciousness with Hurston's outspoken, respectful, lyrical voice when, at the end, Janie is alone in her bedroom and her "thought pictures" become present in Hurston's written words.

By beginning with the utterly impersonal designation, "the woman," for Janie and then moving into an intimate narrative collaboration with her storyteller, Hurston takes on the highly individual, personal characteristics of many oral storytellers. Soon Janie wrests "from menfolk some control of the tribal posture of the storyteller," but her tale does not project the values of Eatonville. Rather, in collaboration with Hurston, she projects a new and different community, first among black women, second among women, and, finally, among women and men. In so doing Janie and Hurston challenge the conventional premises of storytelling as well as the rules governing relationships between women and men. Appropriately, Janie's act of storytelling begins as a private autobiographical act true to her position as an outcast from both the women and men of Eatonville. Her audience consists only of Pheoby who acts as a friend to Janie and, after the tale and her transformation, becomes a bridge between Janie and the estranged community. Janie's voice articulates her unfolding self; her grandmother, Nanny, and her first two husbands, Logan Killicks and Joe Starks, suppress her personality by stifling her right to speak. Only when she meets Tea Cake do voice and self burst openly and strongly into eloquence, and after his death and her return to Eatonville Janie maintains it by virtue of the creative act of storytelling.

Throughout *Their Eyes Were Watching God* Hurston works out the relationship between her voice and Janie's on grounds of cooperation and support—that condition of intimacy sought by women. Hurston frames Janie's storytelling as a necessary action in the struggle for freedom—in this case a struggle for verbal as well as social equality. To succeed, women must change values, not places, and so authorial control is a false premise, a dead letter in the radical context Hurston and Janie build for the word in the world. Instead of having Janie seize authorial control (a sometimes too simple and arbitrary act in fiction and in life), Hurston improvises an intimate rhetoric of call and response. Author and character work together; each shares authorship and authority—collaboratively. Huston wants to show Janie openly and continuously in the round, both as she sees herself and as others see her. So she calls for Janie's story, Janie responds, and the two women, narrator and storyteller, share voices and perspectives throughout the novel.

As the novel flows along, it becomes "more like a conversation than a platform performance," but Hurston opens with a parable uttered in an improvisatory public voice.

> Ships at a distance have every man's wish on board. For some they come in with the tide. For others they sail forever on the horizon, never out of sight, never landing until the Watcher turns his eyes away in resignation, his dreams mocked to death by Time. That is the life of men.
>
> Now, women forget all those things they don't want to remember, and remember everything they don't want to forget. The dream is the truth. Then they act and do things accordingly.

Audibly, Hurston declares that the story about to unfold follows from her reconsideration of the old ways of seeing, living, and telling. About men's dreams she is mockingly metaphorical in high-blown, oratorical tones. About women she is conversational as if to insinuate her intention to abandon authorial control in favor of a more fluid and intimate style of storytelling. Her voice becomes partisan to women's experience as if foretelling that moment in the novel when Janie realizes that her image of her husband Jody "never was the flesh and blood figure of her dreams," and she begins "saving up feelings for some man she had never seen." Like Janie, the woman, Hurston, the storyteller, has "an inside and an outside now"; like Janie, "she knew how not to mix them," and when to mix them. Like

Janie, she is committed to keep the dream alive in imaginative experience. Hurston seeks immensity and intimacy, and from the start, her third-person voice is speculative as well as descriptive, personal as well as impersonal.

Peopled by abstract presences, at first the novel's world seems almost mythical, its space cloudy and inchoate. Although Hurston transforms the void into a particular place, before Janie's entrance Eatonville is without intimacy or immensity. The traditional call-and-response form between individual and community cannot work yet because the men and women of Eatonville are unable to listen or respond openly to Janie's story. They do not share her experience or her values. So, as her first task, Hurston shapes a narrative form responsive to folk and literary traditions, and fluid and improvisational enough to tell Janie's story and inspire a new tradition. By making storytelling and the narrative act collaborative and continuing, she simultaneously launches a new community of values and performs a revolutionary literary act.

Hurston's action-words people the landscape and evoke the moral and social life of Eatonville. But her rich, lyrical imagery is not pastoral or uncritical; she marks the limitations of the community in ways which explain but do not justify its petty response to Janie. The time is sundown, reminiscent of dusk in Toomer's *Cane,* a transitional time for people and nature. Space, too, is transitional, ambiguous, and evasive—half-cosmic, half-historical. "Tongueless, earless, eyeless conveniences all day long," these black folks now "felt powerful and human." Nevertheless, they tell stories and pass judgment jaudiced by the subservience of their days. As a black town, Eatonville is an island surrounded on all sides by tides of racism as treacherous and violent when Janie returns in the twenties as when Hurston grew up there around the turn of the century. The people respond to Janie's self-assertive presence with the bitterness of the oppressed. They make "killing tools out of laughs. It was mass cruelty." There is violence in the people's talk. Their voices assault her, pathetically and vagrantly after she passes the faces behind the words. They prefer an adversarial stance to the intimate responsiveness required to imagine or hear Janie's story.

The revelation of how men and women see Janie relocates Hurston's opening presentation of male and female dreams and prepares for Janie's tale of her struggle for love and autonomy. Still "the woman," Janie may be unidentified but her identity is well-known to all who watch her.

> The men noticed her firm buttocks like she had grape fruits in her hip pockets; the great rope of black hair swinging to her waist and unraveling in the wind like a plume; then her pug-

nacious breasts trying to bore holes in her shirt. They, the men, were saving with the mind what they lost with the eye. The women took the faded shirt and muddy overalls and laid them away for remembrance. It was a weapon against her strength and if it turned out of no significance, still it was a hope that she might fall to their level some day.

The men undress Janie and parse her body according to a lustful male syntax, whereas the women, equally desperate to deny Janie's sexuality, make her field worker's clothes a reductive synecdoche for her person. "But nobody moved, nobody spoke, nobody even thought to swallow spit until after her gate slammed shut." Perhaps because they use words falsely and meanly, without spirit, the onlookers are compelled into lifeless silence by Janie's presence. Not only are these people afraid of the "bossman" by day; at dusk they fear the vital realized self of one of their own who has broken their rules and survived to tell the story. Only after she is out of sight and hearing do they utter their cutting remarks.

The women of the community recede before Janie's actual presence, yet, when she's absent, name her an "ole woman" and demand to know her story. Theirs is a false call. They would have but not hear her story, because in the closed space of their envy they think they know it all already. Only Pheoby remains open both as Janie's friend and as a friend to her story, whatever its gist and whether it confirms or denies her expectations and values. " 'Well, nobody don't know if it's anything to tell or not,' " she tells the townspeople. " 'Me, Ah'm her best friend, and Ah don't know.' " Pheoby is a sympathetic, rigorous audience. Even though she is Janie's "best friend," she won't vouch for her story until she's heard it. Were she to do so before Janie's performance, she would abdicate her right to a full, free response. For her, hearing is believing. Nevertheless, as a friend to Janie and her act of storytelling, Pheoby creates a nest for the story. When Mrs. Sumpkins volunteers to accompany her to Janie's, Pheoby refuses and asserts Janie's right to choose her space and her audience. " 'If she got anything to tell yuh, you'll hear it.' " She then leaves the crowd and goes to Janie. But not at the formal entrance—the front gate. Instead, she "went in at the intimate gate with her heaping plate of mulatto rice." Pheoby makes this entrance deliberately. "Janie must be round the side," she figures, for during Janie's absence Pheoby remains a friend. Though she does not know the particulars of Janie's story, she stays in touch imaginatively, just as Hurston the writer keeps in touch with the thoughts in Pheoby's mind. "Intimate gate," "mulatto rice": these words reify the friendship flowing again between the two women and between them and Hurston, for Huston's rhetorically intimate voice reveals her as a friend to the story. Her narrative *donnée* and Pheoby's personal *donnée* strive for friendship. Hurston knows and does not know her characters, but intimacy requires that she be responsive to their revelations. In this way, all have freedom to come and go. Her characters' minds become part of the narrative space, and Hurston's voice moves easily toward and between the voices of Janie and Pheoby. Theirs is a collaborative eloquence.

Against the grain of Eatonville, Hurston, Janie, and Pheoby evolve a potential community committed to freedom of voice and experience. Janie and Pheoby talk first of small things; each comfortable enough with the other to let the big thing on their minds go for a while. When they do speak of it, they focus on how and whether Janie should tell her story, the framing of the tale rather than the tale. As a friend to Janie, and potentially, though not yet actually, to her story, Pheoby advises her to " 'make hast and tell 'em 'bout you and Tea Cake.' " Pheoby wants to comb the people's curiosity out of her hair; as one of them in her conventional self, she feels accountable. But Janie, who is sufficiently a friend to her story and its telling to resist the prurient interest of Eatonville, understands and accepts Pheoby's position. She is unthreatened by Pheoby's double identity as friend to her and a fully accepted member of the community. True to intimacy, Janie does not ask for total allegiance from Pheoby; in her proud, confident autonomy, she seeks only that fair, open, honest hearing appropriate to friendship. Rather than set ground rules, Janie allows Pheoby the freedom to retell what she'll hear.

Go ahead, " 'You can tell 'em what Ah say if you wants to,' " Janie tells Pheoby. " 'Dat's just de same as me *cause mah tongue is in mah friend's mouf'* " (my italics). Janie's extravagant figure for call and response affirms the intimate sympathetic imagination as an essential faculty for telling someone else's story truly. Because she and Pheoby are friends, Janie trusts Pheoby to be a friend to her story. Janie goes on to tell Pheoby she won't volunteer her story to the people of Eatonville because they have violated the spirit of intimacy. " 'If they wants to see and know, why they don't come kiss and be kissed? Ah could then sit down and tell 'em things.' " Janie proposes civility and courtesy as preconditions for intimacy and the minimum standard for a listener's contribution to storytelling. An audience *earns* the right to hear a story, as Pheoby has done with her acts and words of hospitality and friendship. No one should take for granted the right to hear someone else's story because they live in the same place, or share the same race, gender, or class. Hurston embodies these values for the hearing and telling of stories in the experiential frame she builds for Janie's tale. The common values she and Janie discover as women, as Afro-Americans, and as storytellers inspire genuine call and response.

As Janie's audience, Pheoby departs from convention in another way. As a friend who has heard Janie tell stories before, though not her story, Pheoby asks for help *before* Janie begins her tale:

> "It's hard for me to understand what you mean, de way you tell it. And then again Ah'm hard of understandin' at times."
> "Naw, 'tain't nothin' lak you might think. So 'tain't no use in me telling you somethin' unless Ah give you de understandin' to go 'long wid it. Unless you see de fur, a mink skin ain't no different from a coon hide."

The two women explore the relation between language and experience, speaker and audience. As language, particularly metaphor, expresses the shimmer and radiance of reality, so the dialogue of call and response embodies the flux of human personality. Each individual has responsibilities, and before Janie begins, she tells Pheoby that she depends on her too. She expects her to listen intimately while she tells her story. " 'Pheoby, we been kissin-friends for twenty years, so Ah depend on you for a good thought. And Ah'm talking to you from that standpoint.' " Janie's perspective challenges the impersonality sometimes mistakenly associated with oral storytelling and the authorial control identified with the practice of narrative craft. Janie in her storyteller's dialect and Hurston in her lyrical vernacular agree to look after the needs of the other. Because of their mutual, radical transformation of values, Janie and Hurston, around her not in front of her or behind her, reconstruct the theory and practice of storytelling and narrative.

To underscore the intimate mix of separate and kindred voices as a positive narrative value, Hurston ends the first chapter with a response to Janie's kissing metaphor. "Time makes everything old so the kissing, young darkness became a monstropolous old thing while Janie talked." Hurston animates the cycles of day and night, of individual lives, and of storytelling into concentric circles of meaning and experience. Each moves continuously, palpably, openly, according to its own rhythm and Hurston's polyrhythmic artifice of call and response.

After bearing witness to the conjunction of Janie's storytelling with time's immensity, Hurston invents a companion figure for the spatial scale of Janie's life.

> Janie saw her life like a great tree in leaf with the things suffered, things enjoyed, things done and undone. Dawn and doom was in the branches
>
> "Ah know exactly what Ah got to tell yuh, but it's hard to know where to start at."

Like Pheoby, Hurston enters as a friend to Janie before Janie struggles to utter the first words of her story. But the relation between their two voices depends on "abrupt and unexpected changes." In her remarks on the asymmetry of Negro art, Hurston provides a suggestive description applicable to the polyrhythmic quality present in *Their Eyes Were Watching God.* "There is always rhythm," she observes of African-American music and dancing, "but it is the rhythm of segments. Each unit has a rhythm of its own, but when the whole is assembled it is lacking in symmetry." Likewise, Hurston's juxtaposition of voices highlights what she calls angularity: the African-American determination "to avoid the simple straight line." Sometimes, like the polyrhythms of African and African-American music, the separate voices in *Their Eyes Were Watching God* fuse with one another, but each quickly breaks free and pursues its different individual beat, its own voice line and lifeline.

Although separate, Hurston's and Janie's voices sometimes meet in the space beyond the lines of the text. From images in her character's mind, Hurston composes an extended simile linking Janie's struggle with her story with the tree of life. For Janie's beginning rambles, perhaps because of a sudden fear that, despite Pheoby, she is on her own in storytelling as she was in childhood without the presence of her mother and father. She tells a few anecdotes of girlhood: her unawareness of race (" 'Ah couldn't recognize dat dark chile as me' "); her nickname Alphabet signifying many nullifying names; black children's ridicule of her " 'bout livin' in de white folks backyard' "; her shame at her fugitive father and her resentment at what's left out in accounts of him (" 'Dey didn't tell about how he wuz seen tryin' tuh git in touch wid mah mama later on so he could marry her' "); and, finally, her memory of her grandmother's decision to buy land and a house because she " 'didn't love tuh see me wid mah head hung down.' " At this point Hurston's voice reenters and testifies to the sympathetic effect produced by Pheoby, Janie's immediate audience. "Pheoby's hungry listening helped Janie to tell her story. So she went on thinking back to her young years and explaining them to her friend in soft, easy phrases while all around the house, the night time put on flesh and blackness." Though silent, Pheoby's response to the call of the scarcely begun tale challenges Janie. The intimacy between them nurtures Janie's conventional style ("soft, easy phrases"), and offers Hurston the freedom and narrative space to reconstruct, imagine, and revoice what Janie thinks and feels between the words of the story she tells Pheoby. And in confirmation of the transforming power of their collaboration, the night, too, becomes a sympathetic black presence.

From now on, Hurston and Janie function respectively (and respectfully) as composer and performer of the story. Hurston speaks for Janie because Janie speaks for Hurston too. And Hurston also participates in the intimacy between Janie and Pheoby. Because she writes in a shared, complementary narrative space, Hurston conveys the impression that her embellishments are inspired and sustained by Janie and her spontaneous oral storytelling. Hurston's form also depends on an improvisatory, creative tension, a becoming; her third-person voice is personal but not proprietary. In form and theme, *Their Eyes Were Watching God* pursues the evolving possibilities of intimacy and autonomy. The novel presents Janie's experience and perspective as realities perhaps not yet realized but aspired to on some submerged level of feeling, thought, and speech by black women, women generally, and—such is Hurston's imaginative power—by men as well. For these reasons it is crucial that Hurston's collaborative voice be free to explore not only what Janie said, but things she might have thought but not said, and, not least, that "gulf of formless feelings untouched by thought."

There is another reason for Hurston to break in on Janie's voice and story at this early point. So far, her entrances have framed Janie's tale. To that extent the narrative relationship seems conventional enough. But now Hurston's lyrical tone signals an intimate conversation between her voice and Janie *in the telling* of Janie's story. That is, when Hurston's voice emerges from Janie's chamber of thought and memory, her words testify to a common experience, sometimes lived, sometimes imagined, an experience both women need to articulate. They share what Hurston, describing Janie, calls "that oldest human longing—self-revelation," and referring to her condition before writing *Their Eyes Were Watching God,* described as the "agony" of "bearing an untold story inside you." Hurston realizes that Janie knows her comments to Pheoby about her childhood are an essential prologue to her experience and her tale. "She thought awhile and decided that her conscious life had commenced at Nanny's gate." Reexperienced, those details lead to reconsideration of Janie's "conscious life," and collaboration becomes possible without fear of condescension or control by the author's third-person voice. The form works because Janie stands between Pheoby's immediate responsive silence and Hurston's distanced but intense personal imagination. Finally, Hurston's acknowledgment of "Pheoby's hungry listening" raises the possibility of similar but different responses by a more removed but unremote, potential audience of readers.

III

In *Their Eyes Were Watching God* Hurston and Janie revoice the continuing American/African-American theme of identity. Who am I and how shall I live? And how should a black woman live? To whom does she dare tell her story? These questions pose an old riddle: How does an individual make her voice count in the world, and the world newly present in her words? Especially when other voices work to sustain the status quo of speech and experience, the old patriarchal values. Only with a struggle, and, Hurston's form argues, through collaboration, can Janie resist others' efforts to control her life and, therefore, her story. In the novel human beings inevitably live out one or another version of the word. Janie discovers early and repeatedly that others expect her life and her voice to conform to their text, however contrary it is to her experience and desires. To be free she must formulate her own scripture and learn to be articulate about it in a voice of her own.

And Janie does imagine a text that then becomes accessible and eloquent through a collaboration between her voice and Hurston's. At sixteen, her orgiastic experience of spring inspires an original metaphor, expressed first in Hurston's voice and then directly by Janie when, desperate to make Nanny feel her loathsome nights and days as Logan Killicks's wife, she bursts into verbal bloom: " 'Ah wants things sweet wid mah marriage lak when you sit under a pear tree and think.' " As a young and then an older woman, Janie counters the false calls of Nanny, Logan Killicks, and Starks with a visionary, burgeoning text of her own. Throughout the story her responses to the narrow, belittling, condescending texts of others become a call to her sensuous imagination, a call answered and amplified in the equality of voice and experience she shares with Tea Cake Woods, her third husband. And after his death, her voice, in the act of storytelling, evolves into an instrument able to reach the world and, in more comforting tones, her soul.

No voice is more important than Nanny's in *Their Eyes Were Watching God*. Hers is a black female ancestral text and tale to be absorbed and overcome. Her call begins as a response to Janie's emerging, expectant womanhood and the consequences of her sudden, sensuous, orgiastic communion with the living world. Tragically, Nanny sees only a " 'breath-and-britches,' " " 'trashy nigger' " neighborhood boy " 'lacerating her Janie with a kiss.' " Her call is really a command that Janie marry old Logan Killicks. When Janie protests that " 'he look like some ole skull-head in de grave yard.' " Nanny assaults her verbally, and in response to Janie's pouting, defensive silence, "she slapped the girl violently, and forced her head back so that their eyes met in struggle." In place of intimacy, Nanny resorts to confrontation; in place of call and response, a stringent authorial control. Nonetheless, Nanny's soul presently melts before Janie's "terrible agony," and she stands there "suffering and loving and weeping *internally*, for both of them."

Nanny's sudden rush of sympathy leads her to tell Janie her version of the scheme of things behind the black woman's place in the world. " 'Honey,' " she says, " 'man is de ruler of everything as fur as Ah been able tuh find out. Maybe it's some place way off in de ocean where de black man is in power, but *we don't know nothin' but what we see.* So de white man throw down de load and tell de nigger man tuh pick it up. He pick it up because he have to, but he don't tote it. He hand it to his womenfolks. De nigger woman is de mule uh de world so fur as Ah can see.' " Nanny ends by testifying in a way deceptively like the call and response common to the black church. " 'Ah been prayin' fuh it tuh be different wid you. Lawd, Lawd, Lawd!' " She seems deaf to the fact that for Janie marriage to Killicks is a surrender to the very fate Nanny would protect her from—namely, transformation into " 'de mule uh de world.' " Moreover, Nanny fights Janie's aspirations with a metaphor whose meaning is contradicted by the young woman's sensuous intuitive experience, if not by her lineage. " 'You know, honey, us colored folks is branches without roots,' " Nanny declares, and, lest her words belittle her own strong, stubborn existence, she confides to Janie her dreams of " 'whut a woman oughta be and to do.' " Like many slaves, Nanny saw Emancipation as a beginning: " 'Ah wanted to preach a great sermon about colored women sittin' on high but they wasn't no pulpit for me.' " She hopes her daughter " 'would expound what Ah felt,' " and when she loses the way, Nanny transfers her ambition to Janie, the newest bastard child in her lineage: " 'So whilst Ah was tendin' you of nights Ah said Ah'd save de text for you.' "

Contrary to the view that *Their Eyes Were Watching God* "takes place in a seemingly ahistorical world," Nanny's parable of race follows from the historical context of her experience. As a slave, she was forced into concubinage by her master and bore him a daughter. In his absence his wife threatens to whip Nanny to death and sell the child. Nanny runs away to the swamp and with help from " 'uh friend or two' " hides out until Sherman's army liberates the black folks of Savannah. After the war she refuses offers of marriage and moves to West Florida, but there her daughter's rape by a black schoolteacher destroys her dream of uplift. But not entirely, for Nanny names Janie the successor to her dream. Nanny's capacity for eloquence is clear, but her way of knowing and seeing is narrow and limited. Although she lives somewhat independently and autonomously, perhaps with fatal help from " 'some good white people,' " her life has beaten her down into one of the dimmest flickering sparks later invoked in Janie's folk version of the creation and fall.

In the end, Nanny's eloquence is false and static. Despite all that has happened to her and her daughter, and what she imagines may happen to Janie, her text remains the same. She is content to hand it down to the descendents she assumes will come from Janie and Logan Killicks. She grieves that preaching the " 'great sermon about colored women sittin' on high' " will have to wait, but she sees her time and Janie's governed by unchanging social and historical circumstances. And there is another thing: her text, if experienced, would not transform but merely reverse the past and present inequality between women and men, black women, and white women. For Janie, a rich view of life's possibilities begins with rejection of Nanny's epistemology. And she does overcome the burden of Nanny's expectations. As she retells Nanny's tale, she, along with Hurston, preaches a "great sermon" to Pheoby. But her text is her own, not her grandmother's. Before she learns to speak with conviction and eloquence, she begins to compose her own text, her call to the world. It becomes imperative for her to embody love and autonomy, intimacy and immensity in both her story and her experience. Once her soul reemerges after her marriages to Logan Killicks and Jody Starks, she rejects completely Nanny's text in favor of her desire "to be a pear tree—any tree in bloom" reaching for the "far horizon."

Meanwhile, in the aftermath of her tale, Nanny makes a request calculated to discourage Janie from responding according to her emerging perspective and experience. " 'Have some sympathy fuh me,' " she pleads. " 'Put me down easy, Janie, Ah'm a cracked plate.' " Her sentimental metaphor reinforces Janie's silence. In the days before her marriage to Killicks, Janie keeps unspoken her metaphor about marriage, self, and the pear tree. Instead, she hopes Nanny and the other old folks are right when they tell her that " 'Yes, she would love Logan after they were married.' " But they are wrong, and when Janie comes to tell Nanny, the old woman at first improvises variations on her polar texts: the one of nightmare ("nigger woman de mule uh de world"); the other her dream of "colored women sittin' on high." On the one hand, " 'everybody got tuh tip dey hat tuh you and call you Mis' Killicks,' " she tells Janie; and on the other, " 'Dat's de very prong all us black women gits hung on. Dis love!' " Nanny, though, has escaped this fate, and perhaps that is one reason she softens under the poetry of Janie's newly uttered, womanly text: " 'Ah wants things sweet wid mah marriage lak when you sit under a pear tree and think. Ah. . . .' "

Janie's eloquence and her moving pause compel Nanny to respond with an ambiguous acknowledgment of the possibility of change. " 'Better leave things de way dey is,' " she tells Janie. " 'Youse young yet. *No tellin' what mout happen befo' you die.* Wait awhile, baby. Yo' mind will change' " (my italics). Although Nanny's last words halfheartedly invoke the old certainties, they do not take away the hope she gives Janie. After Nanny dies, largely from her "infinity of conscious pain," Janie waits. She hears "the words of the tress and the wind," and speaks to "falling seeds" as she has heard them speak to each other. The articulate vitality of the living world mocks her static life with Killicks. "She knew now that marriage did not make love. Janie's first dream was dead, so she became a woman."

Through Hurston's voice Janie's unheard words articulate her discovery that for Killicks and, later, Jody Starks, Nanny's text is a code word for women's subservience. Killicks, for instance, eventually gives his young, reluctant wife the choice of satisfying his illusions and desires convincingly if not happily, or chopping wood, plowing, and helping him move manure piles. In the midst of this struggle, Joe Starks comes down the road. To Janie, "he acted like Mr. Washburn or somebody like that," but it is his voice which calls boldly and distinctively—so much so that Hurston, in her continuing collaboration with Janie, makes his voice briefly hers. "Joe Starks was the name, yeah Joe Starks from in and through Georgy. Been workin' for white folks all his life. . . . *He had always wanted to be a big voice,* but de white folks had all de sayso where he come from and everywhere else, exceptin' dis place dat colored folks was buildin' theirselves" (my italics). Now Hurston picks up Janie's mimicry of Joe; without Janie's tale, Hurston could not *do* Joe, but because of their collaboration Hurston fuses these voices in her narration before resuming the past dramatic moment of Janie's encounter with Joe and her recreation of that experience as she tells her tale to Pheoby.

Janie runs off with Starks to escape from the puny straitened space she occupies with Killicks and because Joe "spoke for far horizon." But she is also aware of the things she does not hear in his voice. She "pulled back a long time because he did not represent sun-up and pollen and blooming trees"; in the end she goes because at least "he spoke for change and chance." "With him on it," the seat in the hired rig he takes her away in "sat like some high, ruling chair," but Janies does not notice the echo of Nanny's sermon. Instead, she covers Joe and herself with the sweet pollen of her vision. "From now on until death she was going to have flower dust and springtime sprinkled over everything. A bee for her bloom." Fortunately, Janie keeps in mind the need to adapt her voice to changes in experience. "Her old thoughts were going to come in handy now," Hurston imagines her musing, "but new words would have to be made and said to fit them." The call and response going on so fluidly and implicitly between Hurston and Janie parallels Janie's former readiness to create an original discourse in her marriage to Joe Starks, beginning with her invention of the more intimate name, Jody.

In her life with Starks in the new black town of Eatonville Janie discovers that Jody views her as an appendage. " 'Ah told you in de very first beginning dat Ah aimed tuh be a big voice,' " he reminds her, and follows with a logic antithetical to her vision of reciprocal experience " 'You oughta be glad, 'cause dat makes uh big women outa you.' " Because Joe loves being Mr. Mayor, Janie should gratefully accept the name and identity of Mrs. Mayor. She should live in his space within the sound of his voice. In this context, Janie becomes a listener and absorbs the voices and stories of Eatonville's oral culture, so that later on she and Hurston bring the flowing talk to life in her story. Biding her time, Janie looks for an opening to speak in a circumstance not in the least threatening or competitive to Jody. She finds such an occasion when Jody, overhearing her digust at the mule baiting by the men on the front porch, buys Lum's mule for more than it is worth. " 'Freein' dat mule makes uh mighty big man outa you. Something like George Washington and Lincoln. Abraham Lincoln, he had de whole United States tuh rule so he freed de Negroes. You got uh town so you freed uh mule. You have tuh have power tuh free things and dat makes you lak uh king uh something.' " On the male ritual ground of the *front* porch, Janie's irony is ungrasped by her audience. Only when she tells her tale to Pheoby from the female space of the *back* porch is her audience aware that Janie is calling attention to the unfree condition of women.

Freedom is Janie's text, and her speech of praise enlists Joe in the cause. Her audience of male townspeople salutes her for putting " 'jus de right words tuh our thoughts,' " and Starks "beamed all around, but he never said a word." His silence is significant. It suggests his lack of sympathy with reciprocity or genuine call and response with Janie or anyone else. It also implies embarrassment at Janie's words, for Starks, as he makes clear, expects Janie to sit on high as his possession. Sometimes functional, sometimes ornamental, she is supposed to act and speak at his command; even her psychological inner space should be peopled with his thoughts. A public exchange between him and Janie reveals Starks's perverse reversal of Nanny's text " 'about colored women sittin' on high' ":

> "Somebody got to think for women and chillun and chickens
> and cows. I god, they sho don't think none theirselves."
> "Ah knows uh few things, and womenfolks thinks sometimes
> too."
> "Aw now they don't. They just think they's thinkin'. When
> Ah see one thing Ah understands ten. You see ten things and
> don't understand one."

Such is Joe Starks's absolute rejection and denunciation of Janie's courageous but almost pathetically modest variation on her theme of freedom and reciprocity.

Henceforth, Janie hushes her soul and sustains her womanhood by ceasing to act fully as a woman toward Joe. "The bed was no longer a daisy-field for her and Joe to play in." When a meal of Janie's turns out soggy and tasteless, Joe slaps her hard and humiliatingly across the face, and from that moment she abandons all traces of her quest for intimacy with Joe Starks, instead "saving up feelings for some man she had never seen." In her role as Mrs. Mayor, Janie mostly holds her tongue on the front porch, but when provoked, she proves Joe's and other men's better at verbal combat. On one occasion, tired of hearing variations on Joe's theme of women and chickens, Janie challenges the male voices. " 'Sometimes' " she says, " 'God gits familiar wid us womenfolks too and talks His inside business.' " And she testifies to an intimate conversation with God. " 'He told me how surprised He was 'bout y'all turning out so smart after Him makin' yuh different; and how surprised y'all is goin' tuh be if you ever find out you don't know half as much 'bout us as you think you do.' " Her text warns against male hubris and foreshadows the volcanic potential of her voice as a woman.

Fittingly, given Joe's identity as a public man, the climax of the contention between him and Janie occurs in front of a large audience of mostly male townspeople. Once again, their conflict is expressed on the essential level of maleness and femaleness, but this time Janie plays the dozens in place of her previous attempts to nudge Joe toward reciprocity through an intimate, tentative, conversational response. Now, their words are weapons of war.

> "T'ain't no use in gettin' all mad, Janie, 'cause Ah mention you ain't no young gal no mo'. Nobody in heah ain't lookin' for no wife outa yuh. Old as you is."
> "Naw, Ah ain't no young gal no mo' but den Ah ain't no old woman neither. Ah reckon Ah looks mah age too. But Ah'm uh woman every inch of me, and Ah know it. Dat's uh whole lot more 'n *you* kin say. You big-bellies round here and put out a lot of brag, but t'ain't nothin' to it but yo' big voice. Humph! Talkin' 'bout *me* lookin' old. When you pull down yo' britches, you look lak de change uh life."

Janie does not simply reveal Joe's impotence. Her words proceed from her earlier witty claim that God has told her that women, not men, were the norm at creation. She calls Joe a woman and not a woman like she is, still in the prime of womanhood, but a woman no longer fully a woman. In response Joe can only strike her; henceforth he keeps his distance and relies on other women for comfort in his sickness. When he is near death, Janie breaks the silence between them with tough words which express bluntly the mind that " 'had tuh be squeezed and crowded out tuh make room for yours in me.' " Joe responds with a pathetic command for silence and the wish that lightning strike Janie dead. But she keeps on talking and *her voice* hastens his imminent death.

Starks dies by the text he spoke and lived by, and Janie proclaims it as his epitaph. " 'Dis sittin' in de rulin' chair is been hard on Jody,' she muttered out loud" to no audience but herself; though, in her act of storytelling, Pheoby, and in Hurston's act of narrative, a succession of readers hear her. "She was full of pity for the first time in years," Hurston says. From this moment Janie opposes Nanny's female dream of "colored women sittin' on high" and Jody's male dream of "sittin' in de rulin' chair." Instead, she proposes an experience able to mingle the sensuously intimate "pear tree" with the immensity of "far horizon." For the first time in years Janie looks at herself. Seeing and admiring the "handsome woman" who takes the place of the "young girl" who arrived in Eatonville some twenty-five years before, Janie frees her hair from the kerchief required of her by her late husband. But Janie has learned a thing or two about performance in her role as Mrs. Mayor. So "she starched and ironed her face, forming it into just what people wanted to see"; then, her hair tied back for effect, she issues a public call. "Come heah! Jody is dead. Mah husband is gone from me." Her words are true in different ways for her private and public selves, her past and forthcoming experience, her former and current audiences. Her factual but ambiguous language encourages self-revealing responses from the townspeople, Pheoby, and the rest of us who hear her.

IV

With his "big voice" Joe Starks, in effect, became Nanny's successor, and so it is appropriate that after his death and burial Janie discovers her true feelings about Nanny. Here, as a witness, Hurston tells of Janie's unceasing anger; as a participant in the story she distills a portion of compassion for Nanny, an act impossible for Janie. But only after Hurston helps Janie remove the "cloak of pity" from her feelings is her long-disguised emotion revealed as an abiding hatred. Janie's reasons, spelled out by Hurston, center on her grandmother's transgression of space. "Here Nanny had taken the biggest thing God ever made, the horizon—for no matter how far a person can go the horizon is still way beyond you—and pinched it in to such a little bit of a thing that she could tie it about her granddaughter's neck tight enough to choke her. She hated the old woman who had twisted her so in the name of love." Janie expected intimate allegiance from Nanny. Consequently, Nanny's womanly complicity with the patriarchal scheme of things took special advantage of Janie's girlhood vulnerability. Janie realizes that in her determination to prevent " 'de menfolks white or black" from "makin' a spit cut outa [her],' " Nanny had set her "in the market place to sell," had set her "for still bait" before the repulsive Logan Killicks.

Now, inspired by her experience of Janie's passionate feelings of betrayal, Hurston, without transition, collaborates with Janie on a folk myth of creation and the fall:

> When God had made The Man, he made him out of stuff that sung all the time and glittered all over. Then after that some angels got jealous and chopped him into millions of pieces, but still he glittered and hummed. So they beat him down to nothing but sparks but each little spark had a shine and a song. So they covered each one over with mud. And the lonesomeness in the sparks make them hunt for one another, but the mud is deaf and dumb. Like all the other tumbling mud-balls, Janie had tried to show her shine.

This myth recapitulates the theme of the confining power of those who deny individuals their free human expression. Against the fall, the original damage done, a person has to struggle to keep alive "a shine and a song"— an independent, articulate existence. In fact, Janie's experience calls for revision of this tale as it has the previous texts of Nanny and Joe Starks. Because "the mud is deaf and dumb," the human sparks within need both strong voices and the alert ears of good listeners. To survive and thrive in the world as an articulate presence and personality, Janie (and everyone else) needs to restore and recreate a reciprocal tradition of call and response. To call others and generate a response, an individual has to overcome the deaf-and-dumb proclivity of mud balls—a figure for the unawakened, unresponsive prosaic conventions human beings fall into so easily. So the old tale is a commencement, its possibilities acted out and extended by the collaboration between Hurston and Janie, and perhaps by readers who also seek to show both "a shine and a song."

Meanwhile, a new text of male authorial control is spoken to Janie. " 'Uh woman by herself is uh pitiful thing,' she was told over and again," and such talk is bound up with the townspeople's corollary point that Janie owes her well-being to Joe Starks's money and worldly success. " 'Throwin' away what Joe Starks worked hard tuh git tuhgether,' " Sam Watson tells Pheoby. But Janie has every right to Joe's store and his other worldly possessions; her labor and brains as well as his brought them into existence. Shrewdly, Janie avoids confrontations and commitments in her responses to numerous male suitors. When Pheoby, her new fishing friend, tries to persuade her to marry an undertaker, Janie responds by turning an honest negative into an eloquent positive, " 'Ah jus' loves dis freedom.' " Increasingly, Janie's identity comes not in rebellion against someone else's text but from the pleasure she takes in her reencounter with the world. Left to herself, she will not sit anywhere; hers is to explore, to move out from the sanctum of the pear tree. Alone, at forty, she dreams of integrating the immensity and intimacy of experience in the unfolding story of her life.

When Tea Cake arrives, Janie and her soul are ready; though, with his dark skin, empty pockets, and traveling-man ways, he seems an unlikely candidate for a husband. Easy conversation is the first thing between them. Tea Cake doesn't ask Janie for a match. Instead, he revivifies the thing named: " 'You got a lil piece uh fire over dere, lady.' " He teaches her to play checkers, a game Eatonville convention reserves largely for men, and while they kid around, he performs gently and humorously for her. When he leaves, Janie remembers their intimacy of speech: "Look how she had been able to talk with him right off!" And in her third-person way, Hurston changes once more from a witness to a participant in Janie's inner life. For his part, Tea Cake is a man like Janie is a woman: on the terms of his essential existence and experience. " 'You needs tellin' and showin', and dat's what Ah'm doing,' " he says to Janie after turning up at daybreak to tell her the story of his love. Voice and experience are one for him, and when he definitely, fulsomely declares his love, he makes his words a text of praise. " 'You got de keys to de kingdom,' " he tells her and repeats the refrain after their marriage. For the first time, Janie hears a voice and text celebrate her in her own right, because of who she is. Like her text of the pear tree and far horizon, his embodies autonomy and equality, intimacy and immensity.

When Janie runs off with Joe Starks, she tells herself that "new words would have to be made and said to fit" her "old thoughts." But now telling Pheoby the story of her life with Tea Cake, she says that " 'in the beginnin' new thoughts had tuh be thought and new words said.' " She is right. She calls Tea Cake to think and speak "new words" appropriate to their relationship:

> "So uh aims tuh partake wid everything, hunh?"
> "Yeah, Tea Cake, don't keer what it is."
> "Dat's all Ah wants to know. From now on you'se mah wife
> and mah woman and everything else in de world Ah needs."

For her part, Janie accepts Tea Cake's gambling, violence and all: "It was part of him, so it was all right." In marriage, they talk and work things out mutually and compatibly. They change each other, and, as their love dissolves jealousy and possessive authority, each becomes a freer individual by virtue of their life together.

On the Muck picking beans with Tea Cake in "her blue denim overalls and heavy shoes," Janie "got so she could tell big stories herself from listening to the rest." Moreover, as Janie comes to the Tea Cake section of her story, Hurston's third-person narrative grows increasingly able to mesh with the voices of Janie and the people around her. Again, as if she is more a participant than a witness, Hurston does the townspeople of Eatonville in her vernacular. "Poor Joe Starks. Bet he turns over in his grave every day. Tea Cake and Janie gone hunting. Tea Cake and Janie gone fishing." Equally, Hurston becomes a presence on "the muck" with Janie and Tea Cake: "Wild cane on either side of the road hiding the rest of the world. *People wild too*" (my italics). The inversion suggests that in the act of writing Hurston moves from seeing *what* Janie sees to seeing (and writing) *as* Janie sees (and speaks). Likewise, Hurston modulates without warning into the dialect of the "great flame throwers" on the muck, "handling Big John De

Conquer and his works. How he had done everything big on earth, then went up tuh heben without dying atall." Here and elsewhere, Hurston's diction and rhythm are one with her characters' voices, and then each goes its separate way. The point is that, as in *Mules and Men*, Hurston has been influenced by her characters, so that their oral performances are interwoven with her continuous novelistic act of composition.

Just as Hurston dissolves arbitrary lines of idiom and voice, so Janie crosses lines of class and color in her marriage to the black workingman, Tea Cake. " 'You always did class off,' " Pheoby tells Janie to support her argument against her friend's involvement with Tea Cake. " 'Jody classed me off. Ah didn't,' " Janie responds and in the same conversation argues vehemently against hierarchical demarcations. " 'Dis is uh love game,' " Janie declares and, having earlier faced her feelings about her grandmother, connects the old woman's perspective with the institution of slavery. But she rejects her grandmother's " 'sittin' on porches' " because of her experience. " 'Ah got up on de high stool lak she told me, but Pheoby, Ah done nearly languished tuh death up dere.' " And later on, Janie answers Mrs. Turner's denunciation of Tea Cake and dark Negroes generally. " 'We'se uh mingled people and all of us got black kinfolks as well as yaller kinfolks.' " The mingling spirit imbues Janie's personality and her voice. On all levels of her relationship with Tea Cake, Janie rejects classification for points of being which are fluid. She prefers a contingent over a categorical response to people and the world.

Their Eyes Were Watching God dissolves the hard lines of voice and idiom, gender, class, and color into a vernacular mosaic of language and experience. But it is not always easy or even possible for Janie to integrate the essential, contradictory bits and pieces of assertion and action strewn in her path. Sometimes, the space of the world contains unfamiliar, hostile way stations; at times self is the only home and its only form a chaotic polyrhythmic version of collage. Janie's trial, after she shoots the suddenly, tragically murderous, rabid Tea Cake in self-defense, is such an occasion, and in Hurston's and Janie's hands, a complementary, asymmetrical performance. In the courtroom Janie's intimate experience clashes with the consequences of Jim Crow legal and social space. Reminiscent of the folktale of "Old Sis Goose," judge, jury, and attorneys are all white men. As Janie notices the "eight or ten white women," "nobody's poor white folks" who "had come to look at her," she wishes "she could make *them* know how it was instead of these menfolks." Like the well-to-do white women sitting in front, "all of the colored people standing up in the back of the courtroom" are excluded from participation; they are tolerated only if they remain silent.

That's the institutional context behind Janie's personal hurt when she sees that the black folks, people she and Tea Cake lived among, "were all against her." Without power, they seek refuge in false categories. In life they loved Tea Cake; now in death he seems a hero destroyed by his love for a light-skinned, wealthy woman from a strange place.

To make matters worse and better, the black spectators begin to talk among themselves. They mutter a jaundiced version of the story and insist that justice cannot be done without their participation. "They talked all of a sudden and all together like a choir," in a desperate parody of the black church, "and the top parts of their bodies moved on the rhythm of it." In sympathy with their right to testify, though not with their false story, Hurston's voice briefly flows into their folk speech. But just as quickly, her voice shifts back to a dramatic enactment of the exchange between the prosecutor and Sop-de-Bottom, the spokesperson for Tea Cake's friends. Sop-de-Bottom's emergence is both predictable and appropriate. Back when Tea Cake gives Janie a mostly symbolic beating because he fears losing her and his standing in the community, Sop exclaims: " 'Wouldn't Ah love tuh whip uh tender woman lak Janie!' " A vengeful powerlessness now displaces Sop-de-Bottom's prurient sexual fantasies into a political stance. When he speaks out, "anonymously from the anonymous herd," the state's attorney silences him with a generalized racist threat: " 'Another word out of *you;* out of any of you niggers back there, and I'll bind you over to the big court.' " In ironic confirmation of Hurston's metaphor of "tongues cocked and loaded" as "the only real weapon left to weak folks," " 'Yassuh,' " crawls out as a one-word response to Mr. Prescott.

In this Jim Crow context the bond of community is broken, the participation interrupted between Janie and the other blacks. To Janie, her spirit's survival depends on her ability to make people hear her story. "She was in the courthouse fighting something and it wasn't death. *It was worse than that.* It was lying thoughts" (my italics). She's encouraged to tell her story, rather than simply answer questions put to her. But the actual words are neither spoken nor written by Janie or Hurston in their subsequent acts of storytelling and narrative. Pheoby and, later, Hurston's readers are meant to feel the spell cast on the court by Janie's tale. "She had been through for some time before the judge and the lawyer and the rest seemed to know it." When the spell wears off, those who've listened to Janie fail to see her on her own individual terms, except perhaps for the white women. For if the black folks don't believe what they hear, the white male authorities believe her but do not understand her words. The judge instructs the jury to choose whether Janie is a " 'wanton killer' " or " 'a poor broken creature.' " The fact that she is neither further alienates the blacks. If forced to choose between the two sterotypes, they are willing to regard her as a "wanton killer," but they have participated too much in her life and heard too much of her story to believe that any circumstances, however devastating, would turn her into " 'a poor broken creature.' " Janie remains a free woman, even in this Jim Crow space, by virtue of her voice.

The court's innocent verdict reinforces an opposition between the two groups excluded from the offical judicial process. "And the white women cried and stood around her like a protecting wall and the Negroes, with heads hung down, shuffled out and away." Because they "had realized her feelings," Janie visits the white women "to thank them"; she bears witness to their effort to participate imaginatively in her womanly experience. Later, at the boarding house, Janie overhears the dogmatic, false text preached in a bitter call and response by some black men. " 'Well, long as she don't shoot no white man she kin kill jus' as many niggers as she please,' " one begins. In response, another adds an aphorism which recalls and contradicts Nanny's long ago declaration that " 'de nigger woman is de mule uh de world.' " " 'Well, you know what dey say "uh white man and uh nigger woman is de freest thing on earth." ' " This declaration has nothing to do with Janie or her experience. It falsifies historical reality and denies the oppression of black women by white men not only during slavery but at the very moment this man speaks. It is poison distilled from the bitter spirits of the powerless—the word unrelated to any space outside the abyss of the speaker's mind.

True to her polyrhythmic form, Hurston lets these asymmetrically voiced opinions stand. The very disjointedness testifies to the strength and coherence of Janie's voice. She hears false and bitter accusations yet is undeflected from her grieving, rejuvenating memory of Tea Cake. All else is trivial. Afterward, she invites Tea Cake's friends to the funeral. They come, shamed and apologetic, and Janie quietly makes them welcome. "Sop and his friends had tried to hurt her but she knew it was because they loved Tea Cake and didn't understand." All this is unspoken. Janie does not embellish her story with accounts of reconciliation. Neither does Hurston, and neither does Pheoby intrude on Janie's most vulnerable, intimate thoughts. For Janie, space is peopled now by thoughts more than people. Though Tea Cake's friends beg her to stay on the Muck, she cannot because with him gone, "it was just a great expanse of black mud"—an ooze of silence. She leaves with Tea Cake's package of garden seed in her breast pocket and returns to the place which is closer to home than anywhere else—the space where she unveiled her wings before her flight with him from the branches and blossoms of the pear tree toward sunup and far horizon.

V

The story told but not over, Janie and Pheoby engage in an epilogue of call and response so inviting that when Pheoby leaves, Hurston remains imaginatively in her place. " 'Ah done been tuh de horizon and back,' " Janie tells Pheoby, and her voice testifies to her ability to recover and repeople her former space in Eatonville. Her house, often desolate before when inhabited, is now " 'full uh thoughts, 'specially dat bedroom,' " and those thoughts follow from her experience and her imaginative act of storytelling. Returning to the question of audience with which she began the prologue to her tale, she tells Pheoby to tell the others her story and offers her a little more " 'understandin' to go 'long wid it.' " Preaching a short sermon on love, she begins by renouncing a false, static simile reminiscent of Nanny, Killicks, and Starks: " 'Love ain't somethin' lak uh grindstone dat's de same thing everywhere and do de same thing tuh everything it touch.' " Though a rhetorical straw man, Janie's figure recalls the vision of love and marriage imposed on her experience. But she improvises a new figure: " 'Love is lak de sea. It's uh movin' thing, but still and all, it takes its shape from de shore it meets, and it's different with every shore.' " Janie's words are horizons away from Nanny's text about "sittin' on high"; hers is a sermon of praise for the ebb and flow of love according to the passionate, reciprocal discovery of another *different* personality.

In response, Pheoby announces her transformation of values and self. " 'Ah ain't satisfied wid mahself no mo'. Ah means tuh make Sam take me fishin' wid him after this,' " she declares referring to an action whose small, personal quality signifies genuine, lasting change. She ends on a combative note affirming her intimate, collaborative relationship with Janie: " 'Nobody better not criticize yuh in mah hearing.' " Janie, sensing how fired up Pheoby is, softens her attitude toward the community, Pheoby's prospective audience. " 'Don't feel too mean wid de rest of em,' " Janie advises Pheoby as she hands her " 'de keys to de kingdom' " of storytelling. She does not excuse others in the community for their lack of experience and imagination, but she does remind Pheoby of the limits and possibilities of storytelling. " 'They got tuh find out about livin' fuh theyselves' " are her words, and, as the last words *spoken* in the novel, they remind Pheoby to try to be a friend to her audience as their lives evolve in response to the story she'll tell. A storyteller may launch an audience, but everyone listening journeys to experience on their own.

At this fluid, transitional point, Hurston's voice returns and holds in suspension the serenity of space and time shared by Janie and Pheoby. In their "finished silence" they hear nature's song and story told by "the wind picking at the pine trees" like a blues player—Tea Cake, too, played blues guitar. This is a moment responsive to what Hurston earlier called that "gulf of formless feelings untouched by thought." Janie and Pheoby share an intense intimacy because they have experienced as well as heard the story. Each has been alternately witness and participant in a call and response deepened by Janie's story. But the sea of consciousness is never still. Separate thoughts flow strongly again, and Pheoby goes home to her man and the rhythm of her life, her collaboration with Janie consummated but not ended.

In the "finished silence" of Janie's bedroom, collaboration between her interior voice and Hurston's lyrical voice comes to another, still more intense climax. Hurston's words come and go in harmony with the rhythms of Janie's most intimate images. Suddenly, everything swings in perfect motion as Tea Cake enters the room from Janie's imagination in Hurston's voice. "Every corner of the room," "each and every chair and thing" vibrates "a sobbing sigh." Then "Tea Cake came prancing around her where she was and the song of the sigh flew out of the window and lit in the top of the pine trees." Here and now grief becomes a praise song ("Doncha Know de Road by de Singin' uh de Song?"). The song puts all hurts, including Tea Cake's lapse into beating Janie and her killing act of self-defense, into the cosmic flux of love and life. In the midst of these inarticulate and articulate sounds, Janie realizes that Tea Cake "could never be dead until she herself had finished feeling and thinking."

Janie's presence is Tea Cake's presence, Hurston's presence our presence, and from a most intimate inner voice the last words of *Their Eyes Were Watching God* come to consciousness.

> Here was peace. She pulled in her horizon like a great fish-net. Pulled it from around the waist of the world and draped it over her shoulder. So much of life in its meshes! She called in her soul to come and see.

Together Hurston and Janie reimagine the horizon in a metaphor woven from the threads of Janie's experience. "The net is not the world," Robert Duncan has written; "it is the imagination of the world." Earlier Hurston imagines Janie "getting ready for her great journey to the horizon in search of people"; now, that image of immensity becomes intimate and animate.

The world has a waist, a body, and Janie is a fisherwoman. In memory she catches her life, and sees the forms of the world still becoming, still unfolding in response to her imagination. Janie calls her soul, and in the ending of *Their Eyes Were Watching God,* Hurston calls readers from the written word to the call-and-response pattern on which her text is built.

As a novel, *Their Eyes Were Watching God* is a "great fish-net" whose meshes are woven into a skein of voices. True to a net and a text, there is plenty of open space between the lines. Moreover, Hurston does not intend her voice or her novel to be Janie's voice or Janie's story. Rather, the novel is an "imagination of [Janie's] world"—a net which holds much but not all of "life in its meshes" and then releases its catch back into the sea of consciousness. Equally, the novel is the imagination and experience of voice. In the beginning, Hurston's voice and parable stand alone. But through Janie's act of storytelling and in the act of earned, easeful collaboration between her and Pheoby, her and the other characters, her and Hurston, the novel weaves Hurston's voice into the woof of Janie's "speakerly" dialect, Janie's voice into the warp of Hurston's "writerly" vernacular. Neither voice needs or wants to be dominant, and so authorial control is overthrown in favor of a more equal, democratic idea of voice and form. For as a woman and a novelist, Zora Neale Hurston dreams of love and personality fused in a landscape at once intimate and immense. She dreams also of fiction as a quilt of possibility for both individual and community; fiction able to inspire a tradition of intimate collaboration in literature and experience. In her closing vision of Janie's call to her soul, which not even Pheoby hears but also must imaginne, Hurston calls readers and writers. She calls us all, especially the black women in the audience, to imagine and create a place suitable for our voices, our stories, our lives.

Chronology

?1901	January 7, Zora Neale Hurston born in the all-black town of Eatonville, Florida, to Lucy Ann and John Hurston, a carpenter, minister, and mayor of Eatonville.
1915	Leaves home and begins working as a maid and wardrobe girl for a Gilbert and Sullivan traveling troupe, which eventually brings her to Baltimore, Maryland. There she enters the Morgan College Preparatory School.
1918	Graduates from the Morgan College Preparatory School. Enters Howard University.
1919–24	Studies at Howard under Lorenzo Dow Turner and Alain Locke, who encourage her in her writing.
1920	Receives an associate degree from Howard University.
1921	"John Redding Goes to Sea," Hurston's first published short story, appears in *The Stylus*.
1924	"Drenched in Light" published in *Opportunity* (edited by Charles S. Johnson).
1925	"Spunk" published in *Opportunity*. Granted a scholarship to Barnard College. Moves to New York, and into the center of the Harlem Renaissance.
1925–27	Studies anthropology under Franz Boas (whom she calls "Papa Franz").
1926	"Muttsy" published. Hurston, Langston Hughes, and Wallace Thurman found the short-lived avant-garde magazine *Fire!!*. They regard themselves as rebels, reacting against black leaders such as W. E. B. Du Bois and Alain Locke, who urge that all creative work emphasize the problems between races. Depicting blacks only in relation to white oppression is itself exploitative, Hurston, Hughes, and Thurman say; their first responsibility is to their art.

1927   Hurston undertakes first anthropological field research, going to Alabama for Carter G. Woodson and the Association for the Study of Negro Life and History to interview Cudjo Lewis, an ex-slave. Results published as "Cudjo's Own Story of the Last African Slaves" in the *Journal of Negro History*. (A low point in Hurston's career: though the article includes material of her own, it has since been revealed that it also draws heavily on, perhaps plagiarizes Emma Langdon Roache's *Historic Sketches of the Old South,* published in 1914.) *Great Day,* a play, published. Contract signed with the patron Mrs. Rufus Osgood Mason (whom Hurston calls "God-mother"). Mrs. Mason supports Hurston in anthropological fieldwork in Eatonville, Fla., Alabama, Louisiana, and the West Indies from 1927 to 1932; she insists on owning all of Hurston's material and on approving all uses of it, as she feels Hurston cannot be trusted to manage it properly. Marriage to Herbert Sheen for four months, after a relationship of six years.

1928   Receives B.A. from Barnard College.

1930   "Dance Songs and Tales from the Bahamas" published. Works with Langston Hughes on a play, *Mule Bone,* of which only the third act is published. They quarrel over who is to receive credit for the body of the work, a conflict which is never clearly resolved.

1931   "Hoodoo in America" published. Returns to interview Cudjo Lewis and writes a full-length (unpublished) work based on his life.

1933   "The Gilded Six-Bits" published.

1934   Receives a Rosenwald Fellowship. *Jonah's Gourd Vine,* Hurston's first novel, published. It is praised for its use of folklore and criticized for its lack of a statement on the effects of racism on Southern blacks.

1935   *Mules and Men* published, an anthropological study of the folklore of American blacks. It is the result of intensive participatory research into ceremonies and rituals, and is the first such study written by a black woman. It, too, is praised for its contribution to the knowledge of folklore, but criticized for its lack of political statement.

1936   Receives a Guggenheim Fellowship. Uses it to study folklore in the West Indies.

1937   "Fannie Hurst" published. *Their Eyes Were Watching God* published, perhaps Hurston's most artistically successful work, which was written in seven weeks after a devastating love affair.

1938   *Tell My Horse* published, the first major work on Caribbean folklore.

1939   *Moses, Man of the Mountain* published. Marriage to and separation from Albert Price III, a man several years Hurston's junior. She wrote that her romantic affairs failed at the point when she was expected to give up her work and assume a more traditional role as a wife.

1942   "Story in Harlem Slang" published. *Dust Tracks on a Road,* Hurston's autobiography, published. It is her most commercially successful publication thus far (though perhaps not a factually accurate representation of her life).

1943   "The Pet Negro System," "High John de Conquer," and "Negroes without Self-Pity" published.

1943–46   In this period, Hurston has trouble obtaining funding for her prospective research, a study of blacks in Central America.

1944   "Black Ivory Finale" and "My Most Humiliating Jim Crow Experience" published.

1945   "Beware the Begging Joints" and "Crazy for This Democracy" published. Stricken with a gall bladder and colon infection, a condition which becomes chronic and affects her ability to support herself.

1947   Sails for British Honduras, partially financed by an advance for the novel *Seraph on the Suwanee.*

1948   *Seraph on the Suwanee* published, her first and only novel depicting the lives of whites. Arrested on a morals charge involving a young boy. She was out of the country at the time of the supposed offense and the boy turns out to be psychologically disturbed. The unsubstantiated charges are dropped and she is cleared; but the press, especially the black press, sensationalizes the case. Overwhelmed, she returns to the South, working for a short time as a drama instructor at North Carolina College and as a scriptwriter for Paramount Pictures.

1950   "The Conscience of the Land" and "What White Publishers Won't Print" published. Discovered by a newspaper reporter working as a maid for a wealthy white woman in a fashionable

	section of Miami. She claims that she is researching an article on domestics, but she is living in squalor.
1950–60	Occasional publications during this period, contributions to such journals as *American Legion Magazine,* seem to indicate a growing political conservatism; or an attitude formed growing up in a secure, all-black community. She opposes the 1954 Supreme Court desegregation decision *Brown v. Board of Education,* saying that desegregation implies a degradation of black teachers, students, and schools.
1951	"I Saw Negro Votes Peddled" published. Moves to Eau Gallie, Florida.
1955	Scribner's rejects a manuscript.
1959	Writes and asks Harper and Brothers if they would be interested in publishing a book she is working on, "A Life of Herod the Great." Enters the St. Lucie County Welfare Home in Florida.
1960	Dies without funds to provide for her burial, a resident of the St. Lucie County Welfare Home. She is buried in an unmarked grave in a segregated cemetery in Fort Pierce, Florida.

Contributors

Harold Bloom, Sterling Professor of the Humanities at Yale University, is the author of *The Anxiety of Influence, Poetry and Repression,* and many other volumes of literary criticism. His forthcoming study, *Freud: Transference and Authority,* attempts a full-scale reading of all of Freud's major writings. A MacArthur Prize Fellow, he is general editor of five series of literary criticism published by Chelsea House. During 1987–88, he was appointed Charles Eliot Norton Professor of Poetry at Harvard University.

Robert B. Stepto is a Professor of English, African and Afro-American Studies, and American Studies at Yale University and the author of *From Behind the Veil: A Study of Afro-American Narrative.*

Lorraine Bethel has taught black women's literature and culture at various institutions and was co-editor of the black women's issue of *Conditions.* She is a free-lance editor and writer in New York.

Missy Dehn Kubitschek teaches women's literature at the University of Nebraska in Omaha.

Houston A. Baker, Jr. is the Albert M. Greenfield Professor of Human Relations at the University of Pennsylvania. He is the author of two volumes of poetry and several critical works, including *Long Black Song, The Journey Back,* and *Blues, Ideology, and Afro-American Literature.*

Barbara Johnson is a Professor of French and Comparative Literature at Harvard University. She is the author of *The Critical Difference* and translator of Jacques Derrida's *Disseminations.*

Elizabeth Meese is an Associate Professor of English at the University of Alabama. She has published in *The Kentucky Folklore Record, Boundary 2,* and *American Literature.*

HENRY LOUIS GATES, JR. is a Professor of English, Comparative Literature, and Africana Studies at Cornell University. A MacArthur Prize Fellow, he is the author of *Figures in Black* and *The Signifying Monkey: Toward a Theory of Literary History*.

JOHN F. CALLAHAN is a Professor of English at Lewis and Clarke College in Portland, Oregon. He is the author of *The Illusion of a Nation: Myth and History in the Novels of F. Scott Fitzgerald*.

Bibliography

Bone, Robert. *The Negro Novel in America*. New Haven, Conn.: Yale University Press, 1958.

Bontemps, Arna. *The Harlem Renaissance Remembered*. New York: Dodd, Mead, 1972.

Borders, Florence Edwards. "Zora Neale Hurston: Hidden Woman." *Callalo* 2, no. 2 (May 1979): 89–92.

Brawley, Benjamin. *The Negro Genius*. New York: Dodd, Mead, 1937.

Brown, Sterling A. "Luck Is a Fortune." *The Nation*, 16 October 1937.

Byrd, James W. "Zora Neale Hurston: A Novel Folklorist." *Tennessee Folklore Society Bulletin* 21 (1955): 37–41.

Christian, Barbara. *Black Feminist Criticism*. New York: Pergamon, 1985.

———. *Black Women Novelists*. Westport, Conn.: Greenwood, 1980.

Cooke, Michael G. "The Beginnings of Self-Realization." In *Afro-American Literature in the Twentieth Century*, 71–84. New Haven, Conn.: Yale University Press, 1984.

Ferguson, Otis. "You Can't Hear Their Voices." *The New Republic* 92 (13 October 1937): 276.

Ford, Nick Aaron. *The Contemporary Negro Novel: A Study in Race Relations*. College Park, Md.: McGrath, 1936.

Gates, Henry Louis, Jr., ed. *Black Literature and Literary Theory*. New York: Methuen, 1984.

Gayle, Addison, Jr. "The Outsider." In *The Way of the New World: The Black Novel in America*, 139–150. Garden City: Anchor, 1975.

Giles, James R. "The Significance of Time in Zora Neale Hurston's *Their Eyes Were Watching God*." *Negro American Literature Forum* 6, no. 2 (Summer 1972): 52–3, 60.

Gloster, Hugh M. "Zora Neale Hurston: Novelist and Folklorist." *Phylon* 4 (1943): 153–59.

Helmick, Evelyn T. "Zora Neale Hurston." *The Carrell* 2 (June–December 1970): 1–19.

Hemenway, Robert E. *Zora Neale Hurston: A Literary Biography*. Urbana: University of Illinois Press, 1977.

Howard, Lillie P. " 'Them Big Old Lies.' " *Callalo* 2, no. 2 (May 1979): 95–97.

———. *Zora Neale Hurston*. Twayne World Authors Series. Boston: G. K. Hall, 1980.

Huggins, Nathan. *Harlem Renaissance*. New York: Oxford University Press, 1971.

Hughes, Carl Milton. *The Negro Novelist*. New York: Citadel, 1953.

Hughes, Langston. *The Big Sea*. New York: Hill & Wang, 1963.

Hull, Gloria T. "Rewriting Afro-American Literature: A Case for Black Women Writers." *Radical Teacher* 6 (December 1977): 10–14.

Jordan, June. "On Richard Wright and Zora Neale Hurston: Notes Toward a Balancing of Love and Hatred." *Black World* 23, no. 10 (August 1974): 4–8.

Kilson, Marion. "The Transformation of Eatonville's Ethnographer." *Phylon* 33 (1972): 112–19.

Kunitz, Stanley, and Howard Haycraft. *Twentieth-Century Authors*. New York: H. W. Wilson, 1972.

Lee, Valerie Gray. "The Use of Folktalk in Novels by Black Women Writers." *CLA Journal* 23 (March 1980): 266–72.

Locke, Alain. "Jingo, Counter-Jingo and Us." *Opportunity* 16, no. 1 (January 1938): 8–10.

Love, Theresa. "Zora Neale Hurston's America." *Papers on Language and Literature* 12 (1976): 422–37.

Marks, Donald R. "Sex, Violence and Organic Consciousness in Zora Neale Hurston's *Their Eyes Were Watching God*." *Black American Literature Forum* 19, no. 4 (Winter 1985): 152–57.

McCredie, Wendy J. "Authority and Authorization in *Their Eyes Were Watching God*." *Black American Literature Forum* 16, no. 1 (Spring 1982): 25–28.

Neal, Larry. "A Profile: Zora Neale Hurston." *Southern Exposure* 1, nos. 3–4 (Winter 1974): 163–64.

Perry, Margaret. *Silence to the Drums: A Survey of the Literature of the Harlem Renaissance*. Westport, Conn: Greenwood, 1976.

Rambeau, James. "The Fiction of Zora Neale Hurston." *The Markham Review* 5 (Summer 1976): 61–64.

Rayson, Anne L. "The Novels of Zora Neale Hurston." *Studies in Black Literature* 5, no. 3 (Winter 1974): 1–10.

Rosenblatt, Roger. "Eccentricities." In *Black Fiction*, 84–90. Cambridge: Harvard University Press, 1974.

Schraufnagel, Noel. *From Apology to Protest: The Black American Novel*. Deland, Fla.: Everett, Edwards, 1973.

Schwalbenberg, Peter. "Time as Point of View in Zora Neale Hurston's *Their Eyes Were Watching God*." *Negro American Literature Forum* 10, no. 3 (Fall 1976): 104–5, 107–8.

Smith, Barbara. "Sexual Politics and the Fiction of Zora Neale Hurston." *Radical Teacher* 8 (May 1978): 26–30.

Southerland, Ellease. "Zora Neale Hurston: The Novelist-Anthropologist's Life/Works." *Black World* 23, no. 10 (August 1974): 20–27.

Starke, Catherine Juanita. *Black Portraiture in American Fiction*. New York: Basic Books, 1971.

Stepto, Robert B. *From Behind the Veil: A Study of Afro-American Narrative*. Urbana: University of Illinois Press, 1979.

Stevens, George. "Negroes by Themselves." *Saturday Review of Literature* 16, no. 21 (September, 1937): 3.

Turner, Darwin. *In a Minor Chord.* Carbondale: Southern Illinois University Press, 1971.

Walker, Alice. *In Search of Our Mother's Gardens: Womanist Prose.* New York: Harcourt Brace Jovanovich, 1983.

Walker, S. Jay. "Zora Neale Hurston's *Their Eyes Were Watching God:* Black Novel of Sexism." *Modern Fiction Studies* 20 (Winter 1974–75): 519–28.

Wall, Cheryl A. "Zora Neale Hurston: Changing Her Own Words." In *American Novelists Revisited,* edited by Fritz Fleishmann, 371–89. Boston: G. K. Hall, 1982.

Washington, Mary Helen. "The Black Woman's Search for Identity." *Black World* 21, no. 10 (August 1972): 68–75.

Williams, Sherley Anne. Foreword to *Their Eyes Were Watching God,* by Zora Neale Hurston. Urbana: University of Illinois Press, 1978.

Wright, Richard. "Between Laughter and Tears." *The New Masses* 25, no. 2 (5 October 1937): 22–25.

Young, James O. *Black Writers of the Thirties.* Baton Rouge: Louisiana State University Press, 1973.

Acknowledgments

"Ascent, Immersion, Narration" by Robert B. Stepto from *From Behind the Veil: A Study of Afro-American Narrative* by Robert B. Stepto, © 1979 by the Board of Trustees of the University of Illinois. Reprinted by permission of the University of Illinois Press.

" 'This Infinity of Conscious Pain': Zora Neale Hurston and the Black Female Literary Tradition" by Lorraine Bethel from *All the Women Are White, All the Blacks Are Men, But Some of Us Are Brave: Black Women's Studies*, edited by Gloria T. Hull, Patricia Bell Scott, and Barbara Smith, © 1982 by the Feminist Press and Gloia T. Hull, Patricia Bell Scott, and Barbara Smith. Reprinted by permission.

" 'Tuh de Horizon and Back': The Female Quest in *Their Eyes Were Watching God*" by Missy Dehn Kubitschek from *Black American Literature Forum* 17, no. 3 (Fall 1983), © 1983 by Indiana State University. Reprinted by permission.

"Ideology and Narrative Form" (originally entitled "Figurations for a New American Literary History") by Houston A. Baker, Jr. from *Blues, Ideology, and Afro-American Literature: A Vernacular Theory* by Houston A. Baker, Jr., © 1984 by the University of Chicago. Reprinted by permission of the University of Chicago Press.

"Metaphor, Metonymy and Voice" (originally entitled "Metaphor, Metonymy and Voice in *Their Eyes Were Watching God*") by Barbara Johnson from *Black Literature and Literary Theory*, edited by Henry Louis Gates, Jr., © 1984 by Methuen & Co. Ltd. Reprinted by permission.

"Orality and Textuality in *Their Eyes Were Watching God*" (originally entitled "Orality and Textuality in Zora Neale Hurston's *Their Eyes Were Watching God*") by Elizabeth A. Meese from *Crossing the Double Cross: The Practice of Feminist Criticism* by Elizabeth A. Meese, © 1986 by the University of North Carolina Press. Reprinted by permission.

"A Black and Idiomatic Free Indirect Discourse" (originally entitled "Talking Books: A Black and Idiomatic Free Indirect Discourse") by Henry Louis

Gates, Jr., and Barbara Johnson from *Reading Zora: Discourse and Rhetoric in Their Eyes Were Watching God* by Henry Louis Gates, Jr., and Barbara Johnson, © 1987 by Henry Louis Gates, Jr., and Barbara Johnson. Reprinted by permission of Brandt & Brandt, Inc.

" 'Mah Tongue Is in Mah Friend's Mouf': The Rhetoric of Intimacy and Immensity in *Their Eyes Were Watching God*" by John F. Callahan, © 1987 by John F. Callahan. Published for the first time in this volume. Printed by permission.

Index